Friendship and Other Weapons

by the same author

How to Be Angry
An Assertive Anger Expression Group Guide for Kids and Teens
Signe Whitson
Foreword by Dr Nicholas Long
ISBN 978 1 84905 867 4

of related interest

Cyberbullying
Activities to Help Children and Teens to Stay Safe in a Texting,
Twittering, Social Networking World
Vanessa Rogers
ISBN 978 1 84905 105 7

Rising Above Bullying
From Despair to Recovery
Carrie Herbert and Rosemary Hayes
Foreword by Esther Rantzen
Illustrated by Roxana de Rond
ISBN 978 1 84905 123 1

Bully Blocking
Six Secrets to Help Children Deal with Teasing and Bullying
Revised Edition
Evelyn M. Field
ISBN 978 1 84310 554 1

Games and Activities for Exploring Feelings
Vanessa Rogers
ISBN 978 1 84905 222 1

Creativity Unleashed
Therapeutic Activities and Character Education Ideas for Working with Children and Teens
Lindsey Joiner
ISBN 978 1 84905 865 0

Helping Children to Cope with Change, Stress and Anxiety
A Photocopiable Activities Book
Deborah M. Plummer
Illustrated by Alice Harper
ISBN 978 1 84310 960 0

Helping Children to Build Self-Esteem
A Photocopiable Activities Book
2nd edition
Deborah M. Plummer
Illustrated by Alice Harper
ISBN 978 1 84310 488 9

Friendship and Other Weapons

Group Activities to Help Young Girls Aged 5–11 to Cope with Bullying

Signe Whitson

Jessica Kingsley *Publishers*
London and Philadelphia

The idea for the *Linking Arms* activity (page 90) was originally developed by the University of Michigan's Strong Moms-Strong Girls group curriculum. Adapted with permission.

First published in 2012
by Jessica Kingsley Publishers
116 Pentonville Road
London N1 9JB, UK
and
400 Market Street, Suite 400
Philadelphia, PA 19106, USA

www.jkp.com

Library of Congress Cataloging in Publication Data
Whitson, Signe.
  Friendship and other weapons : group activities to help young girls aged 5--
11 to cope with bullying / Signe Whitson.
      p. cm.
  Includes bibliographical references.
  ISBN 978-1-84905-875-9 (alk. paper)
  1. Friendship in children. 2. Bullying--Prevention. 3. Group counseling
for girls. 4. Girls--Psychology. I. Title.
  BF723.F68W45 2012
  302.3'408342--dc23
                        2011020219

British Library Cataloguing in Publication Data
A CIP catalogue record for this book is available from the British Library

ISBN 978 1 84905 875 9
eISBN 978 0 85700 540 3

Printed and bound in the United States

For Hannah and Elle:

May you always have the confidence to make

your voices heard and the knowledge that I

will be there to listen and to love you

Contents

Session 3

Silent Whispers: Two Rules for Stopping Gossip

Session 4

The Red Flags of Girl Bullying: When Friendship Is Used as a Weapon

Supplementary Session 3 24/7 Contact: Guidelines for Texting, IMing, and Facebook

Introduction

About this book

Welcome to the world of little girls! It begins as such a lovely place, where heart and rainbow doodles adorn notebook covers, best friendships are formed within seconds, and bold, exuberant voices carry squeals of carefree laughter and brazen delight. Emotions are unabashedly shared among young girls; happiness is worn on a sleeve and anger is voiced with authentic candor.

But length-of-stay in this accepting, kindly world is time-limited for many girls in their earliest school years. Seemingly overnight, sweet sentiments like, "I love your dress," turn into thinly veiled criticisms such as, "Why are you wearing *that* dress?" Long before most school programs begin anti-bullying campaigns, young girls are getting a full education in social aggression.

Publicly displayed doodles become private, gossip-filled notes passed exclusively between BFFs (the coveted Best Friends Forever designation). BFFs cut ties through wordless gestures that are heard loud and clear. Celebratory birthday parties become cruel tools of exclusion as young girls use guest lists to exact power and express revenge.

There is no warning sign or rite of passage to mark the transition into this new era of relationships, nor do girls receive a formal education in how to cope when friendships are suddenly wielded as weapons. In fact, the very danger presented by this new culture is its silence. Rachel Simmons (2009) explains that the social norms of a young girl's world dictate that anger and conflict cannot be voiced directly, so this powerful emotion is concealed behind an angry smile and conflict is waged in ruthlessly passive aggressive ways (Long, Long and Whitson 2009).

Young girls do not ask for admission to this new culture, yet few can escape its day-to-day realities. By the early school years, most girls have experienced unspoken—but not unsubtle—acts of relational aggression that shake the carefully laid foundations of their self-image, personal values, and beliefs about friendship.

How can professionals and parents prepare young girls for their inevitable experiences with girl bullying, disguised as friendship?

No child should have to find their way through the friendship challenges of the early school years alone. *Friendship and Other Weapons* provides counselors, social workers, educators, youth workers, and parents with step-by-step directions, activities, guidance, and information for preparing small groups of early school-aged girls to successfully traverse the winding, and seemingly endless roads of friendship.

Friendship and Other Weapons is about breaking the code of silence that governs conflict in the early school years. By creating safe, open, and fun forums in which girls can talk, learn, and compare experiences, participants gain new skills for speaking up when it comes to expressing their feelings and confidence for confronting incidents of cruelty disguised as friendship.

Friendship and Other Weapons helps preserve the exuberant, confident voices of young girls and strengthen their skills to assertively express their thoughts and feelings in ways that respect others, reject bullying behavior, and reflect important values such as empathy, kindness, cooperation, connectedness, personal responsibility, and self-respect. Based on thought-provoking discussions, engaging games, strength-discovering exercises, and confidence-boosting fun, the hands-on activities in *Friendship and Other Weapons* build critical knowledge and friendship survival skills such as:

- recognizing the red flags of girl bullying
- responding assertively to bullying behavior
- realizing personal strengths
- connecting with healthy friendships
- becoming an ally to others facing bullying
- resolving conflicts directly
- using technology and social media ethically
- reaching out to trustworthy adults
- making values-based decisions.

Who is Friendship and Other Weapons for?

The early school years are a critical window of time in the social and emotional development of young girls. Parents, teachers, counselors, and other trustworthy adults are still highly influential at this age, and in an ideal position to shape a girl's thoughts, feelings, and behaviors when it comes to social aggression and bullying (Anthony and Lindert 2010). *Friendship and Other Weapons* gives caring adults a detailed roadmap and realistic resources for guiding girls through this unique period of their development.

Education professionals

The group curriculum is written for teachers, school social workers, guidance counselors, and educational support personnel to conduct the sessions with small groups of girls and encourage open dialogue about everyday friendship challenges. While lingering social norms may discourage girls from acknowledging conflict or expressing anger, *Friendship and Other Weapons* exposes masked aggression and frees young girls to express themselves with assertive candor.

Mental health professionals

Clinical social workers, psychologists, and licensed professional counselors employed in residential youth care, group homes, outpatient, and other mental health settings will be interested in *Friendship and Other Weapons* as a complete, ready-to-use 12-session group guide that offers specific objectives and detailed lesson plans for working with young girls who are learning about the nature of real friendship. Using realistic role plays, engaging games, thought-provoking discussions, and creative expression outlets, the curriculum helps professionals tailor each session to the needs, interests, and ability levels of group participants.

Recreational group leaders

Girls benefit from having a supportive network of trustworthy adults who are informed about the nature of girl bullying and open to meaningful dialogue about real friendship. Leaders of afterschool programs, Girl Scout troops, sports teams, religious organizations, and youth-oriented community groups will find the activities and discussions in the *Friendship and Other Weapons* curriculum very well suited for their individual and group interactions with girls.

Parents and caregivers

Parents and caregivers can use *Friendship and Other Weapons* as a tool for understanding the day-to-day friendship challenges faced by their young daughters. Each session of the group curriculum features a *Letter to Parents*, which includes a summary of the session's activities as well as ideas for at-home discussions that help parents pick up where group discussions leave off.

Parents whose daughters are not taking part in a group experience can adapt the activity and discussion topics for one-on-one use. While girls gain from discussing friendship issues with one another, being able to talk about the nature of girl bullying and friendship challenges with parents is also critical.

Parents often struggle with the question of, "Should I intervene in my daughter's friendship problems?" The line between helicopter and hands-off parenting can get confusing, as adults waver between wanting to protect their daughters from any kind of hurt and believing that girl fighting is an inevitable rite of passage. The bottom line is this: girls need to make peace with conflict and they need adult help to do it (Simmons 2002, p.231).

The *Friendship and Other Weapons* curriculum provides girls with the knowledge and skills to recognize and effectively respond to girl bullying behavior. When these lessons are reinforced at home, parents validate the emotional experiences of their daughters and complete the circle of supportive adult guidance when it comes to learning how to cope with bullying.

For information about mother–daughter workshops based on the lessons in the *Friendship and Other Weapons* curriculum, please visit www.signewhitson.com.

Girls!

Most of all, the group activities in this book are designed to reach out to girls in the early school years and provide them with an open, safe, fun forum to talk about the nature of conflict and to learn skills for fostering real friendships.

While the book title *Friendship and Other Weapons* is used to convey to adult readers the nature of how girl bullying is acted out within relationships, girl participants will come to know their membership as part of a *Real Friendship* group. As such, the solution-focused lessons, engaging group activities, and relevant discussions will help girls recognize the masked tactics of girl bullying and respond to them in honest, relationship-enhancing, self-affirming ways.

Facilitator qualifications

Friendship and Other Weapons is written as a step-by-step facilitation guide so that any adult with professional training in teaching and/or working with young people can lead the group. Facilitators of all experience levels should be sure to thoroughly read the entire curriculum before beginning the group and should review and prepare the materials prior to each session. Newcomers to group facilitation will benefit from co-leading the session with another adult to observe and learn the finer points of group process.

Please note: The same adult(s) should facilitate the group session after session. The group process will be less effective if different adults lead the sessions. Both continuity and the sense of group cohesion are compromised when leadership is inconsistent.

Creating a positive group environment

Young people do some of their very best learning within small groups. When girls are able to come together to discuss friendship values, increase awareness of girl bullying behaviors, and learn skills for standing up to bullying, they benefit from knowing that they are not alone. Group participants feel supported by peers who are 'all-in-the-same-boat' (Shulman 2008) and profit from practicing new skills on real-world peers.

The facilitator can foster trust and help create a positive group environment by:

- role modeling assertive behaviors in all interactions with group members

- demonstrating unconditional positive regard for each participant

- conveying a belief in the abilities and skills of individual members and the group as a whole

- customizing the curriculum to the needs of the group

- encouraging active participation

- providing regular feedback to individual members

- safeguarding participants from hurtful interactions

- asking group members for their opinions and feedback

- celebrating group learning and successes.

Using the curriculum

Friendship and Other Weapons is a complete, ready-to-use curriculum. Each session begins by outlining specific learning objectives for participants and provides a list of necessary materials and *Before beginning* preparations.

Detailed, step-by-step instructions are provided to the facilitator for each session, along with italicized suggestions for general wording and important messages to convey to participants. Following the instructions for each session, facilitators will find handouts, activities, and *Friendship Journal* pages that can be photocopied and distributed to group participants.

Several of the sessions utilize role plays, scenarios, and/or questions pre-printed on index cards, for distribution to participants. It may be helpful for the facilitator to prepare extra cards in order to customize the activities with relevant real-world examples and provide a variety of options that encourage maximum participation from group members.

Supplementary activities

Following the regular 12-session curriculum, there is a Supplementary Activities section that features optional activities and discussions for helping young girls survive and thrive in a social media world. Three distinct topic areas focus on song lyrics and music video content, entertainment and advertising imagery, and guidelines for texting and social media use. The activities in this section may be incorporated into the regular 12-session curriculum or used separately, on an as-needed basis.

While not all of the girls for whom the *Friendship and Other Weapons* curriculum is designed are old enough to have cell phones or use social media, it is a near-certainty that all girls will be exposed to this world at an early age. The discussions and activities in this supplementary section provide an open forum for girls to talk about media use and to think critically about media messages.

Time requirements

Each session in the *Friendship and Other Weapons* curriculum is designed to be completed in about 45 minutes, though this time frame is offered only as a guideline. Depending on the program schedule, the day, the group, and the mood (among other variables), some discussions will need more or less time. Sessions can be divided and continued at later points, especially for younger participants who need additional time to learn and process new information. Skills that require extra practice (e.g. *STANding up to Bullying*) may also necessitate additional time. The facilitator should use discretion in guiding the girls through each lesson, taking care to make the atmosphere interesting and fun and, most importantly, allowing each child to feel heard and understood.

Scheduling

Whenever possible, schedule the group sessions at regular intervals. Kids benefit from the predictability of knowing when sessions will take place and come to look forward to the regular interactions. Also, avoid holding the *Real Friendship* sessions during times of day when participants will be likely to have to come and go or miss frequent sessions. It is frustrating for young people to begin addressing a topic but not have the opportunity to finish it. Likewise, it is disruptive to the group process for the membership to be inconsistent. When adults prioritize group time, they signal to participants that the curriculum is important and convey their commitment to participants' learning.

The group room

Along with dedicating regular time to the group, it is helpful to select a physical space that accommodates group members comfortably and allows enough space for movement around the room during group activities. Additionally, it is important to use a room that is free of noisy distractions and provides enough privacy for participants to feel safe engaging in honest self-reflection and discussion.

Group size

Because each session is built largely around group activities and discussions, the ideal group size is 6–10 girls per adult facilitator. Whenever possible, enough adults should be present to allow each of the girls the chance to feel heard and understood and to be sure that all concerns, questions, and issues receive due attention.

Age of group members

The discussions and activities of the *Real Friendship* group are designed to be used with girls ages 5–11. There will likely be instances in which some girls are able to move quickly through concepts while others may need more focus and explanation. Each session has a special *Customizing the curriculum* section that provides notes on adapting the lessons for varied ages, ability levels, and real-world experiences. Since this is designed as a group experience, the facilitator will be called upon to use his or her skill to make the material meaningful for all.

Arranging girls into pairs and small groups for group activities and discussions

Because developing supportive friendships is a primary goal of this group, it is critical that the facilitator sets the tone for open and inclusive relationships. Whenever partners or small groups are needed, the facilitator should play a role in group formation and take care to protect girls from experiences of exclusion.

An easy and conflict-free way of doing this is to use the *Craft Stick Method*. Simply write the name of each participant on a popsicle (ice lolly) stick prior to the first group session. Anytime pairs or small groups need to be formed, the facilitator can draw from the pre-printed sticks and establish groups randomly. Index cards that kids decorate and personalize also work well for this group formation method.

Group materials

Many of the *Real Friendship* sessions involve handouts that are completed during the group and can serve as helpful "take home" reminders of specific skills. Every group session suggests a *Friendship Journal* topic for participants to continue their reflection outside of group. It is helpful to provide participants with a folder in which they can keep all of their *Real Friendship* papers.

Session 1

Words Matter!
Establishing the Ground Rules for Real Friendship

Session objectives

- To introduce the purpose and format of the *Real Friendship* group sessions.

- To set the tone for an engaging, practical, respectful, and fun group experience.

- To compare the destructive impact of insults (*Shredders*) with the self-esteem building effects of kind words (*Builders*) and to commit to using kind words to enhance friendships.

Materials needed

- flipchart paper and markers (a chalkboard, dry erase board, or any other visible way to record participant answers will work equally well. Throughout this book, we will use the term "flipchart" for simplicity's sake)

- Jenga® or other children's building blocks

- (optional) a folder for each participant, to store group handouts and *Journal* pages from session to session.

Before beginning

- Pre-print the words "*Feelings*" or "*Self-esteem*" on a piece of flipchart paper.

- Prepare copies of the *Friendship Journal* (page 33) for each participant.

- Prepare copies of the *Letter to Parents* handout (page 34) for each participant to take home.

Welcome to the group

1. Welcome each participant to the first session of the *Real Friendship* group and offer a brief introduction about the purpose of the group. In your own words, share the following:

    ○ *Friendships are an important part of being a kid. When friendships are going well, they make life fun and can help girls to feel good about themselves. When they are going badly, it is normal to feel sad, angry, lonely, and even confused about what has gone wrong.*

    ○ *This 12-week group experience is designed to teach girls how to enjoy* Real Friendship *as a way of caring for others and feeling good about themselves. Through games, activities, and group discussions, we will learn everyday ways that friendship can be used to make life better. At the same time, we will be practicing steps to make sure that friendship is never misused as a weapon that causes sadness or hurt.*

    ○ *This group is all about encouraging girls to express thoughts and feelings openly and directly. Your opinions matter and your participation is highly valued. Please know that your voice is important and you are encouraged to speak your mind honestly and often.*

2. Introduce yourself, if the participants do not already know you. Share a bit about your interest in helping girls develop skills for using friendship in supportive ways that contribute to healthy relationships and positive self-esteem.

3. If you will have any co-facilitators assisting you with the group, allow them to introduce themselves at this point.

Opening activity: Coming Together as a Group

Even in groups where kids know each other well, it is important to allow for an "opening activity" period each session in which girls can get out of a school/session/treatment mindset and into group mode.

The primary purpose of this first group session is to lay the foundation for a safe and fun atmosphere in which girls can get to know each other and begin to form a trusting group identity. This icebreaker helps the girls work toward these goals.

1. Explain the rules as follows:

    ○ *When I say "Go," begin walking around the room.*

- *I will ask several questions aloud. Determine your individual answer to the question and join with the other girls in the room who have the same answer.*

- *Take some time to talk with the members of your small group. When you hear the next question, it is time to move on to a new group.*

2. When you are confident that all of the girls understand the activity rules, allow the girls to begin mingling.

3. Ask enough questions to get the girls to group and regroup themselves 3–4 times. Suggestions for good questions include:

- *When you brush your teeth, do you start with your top teeth or your bottom ones?* (Two distinct groups should form.)

- *Do you write with your left hand or your right one?* (Two distinct groups should form.)

- *When it comes to ice cream, do you prefer chocolate, vanilla, or strawberry?* (Three distinct groups should form.)

- *In your family, are you the oldest child, youngest child, or somewhere in the middle?* (Three distinct groups should form.)

- *What color eyes do you have?* (Expect 4–5 groups, including blue, green, hazel, brown, and black eye color.)

- *What is your favorite color?* (Expect multiple groups.)

4. Once the girls have had the opportunity to interact within 3–4 different sub-groups, ask a question that you are certain all of the girls will answer in common, such as:

- *Do you attend* [name of school]?

- *Are you under 12 years old?*

- *What planet do you live on?*

- *Did you wake up this morning?*

5. Emphasize that in any group of girls, members will share things in common and have differences as well:

- *One of the most enjoyable things about friendship is talking to one another and learning all of the things that make us alike and different.*

- *It is important to always keep in mind that no matter how many categories we list and different preferences we identify, in the end, we all come together as one single group.*

○ *Since we will spend our group time talking about friendships and working together, let's create a set of ground rules for how we should treat one another and enjoy our sessions.*

Group ground rules

Ground rules help participants understand what is expected of them in the group setting and also understand how the *Real Friendship* group will function differently than a school classroom or sports team.

- In your own words, explain the importance of establishing group ground rules:

  ○ *Ground rules are expectations for how we behave in the group and how we treat one another.*

  ○ *The rules we establish can help us feel safe by letting all of us know the purpose and the limits of the group, including what is expected and what is not permitted.*

- Write *"Real Friendship Group Rules"* at the top of a large piece of flipchart paper. Encourage girls to brainstorm ground rules.

- Examples of helpful group ground rules are statements like:

  ○ *Maintain the confidentiality of what is shared in the group.*

  ○ *Don't talk while others are talking.*

  ○ *This is a judgment-free zone! We are here to support and encourage one another.*

- In establishing group ground rules, it is most effective to have girls come up with the majority of the rules.

  ○ Usually, kids generate very good rules. The facilitator should intervene only if a rule is completely off-base.

  ○ Intervene by asking other group members what they think about a rule or, in a non-judgmental way, talk about why the rule might not work well in the group.

  ○ If important rules are omitted by the kids, suggest them at the end of the brainstorming.

- Post the *Real Friendship Group Rules* in a prominent location in the group room and let the girls know that the group rules will be in effect throughout every session.

Shredders and Builders

1. Explain the *Shredders and Builders* activity:

    ◦ *One thing that is very clear from our discussion about* Real Friendship Group Rules *is that the way we treat one another matters when it comes to friendship and feeling good about ourselves.*

    ◦ *This next activity shows just how true this is.*

2. Ask for 2–3 volunteers to give a definition of an "insult." Affirm all responses, emphasizing that insults are words and behaviors intended to hurt someone's feelings or make them feel badly. In this group, we will be referring to insults as "*Shredders*" because of how they can shred a person's feelings and self-confidence.

3. Ask for a volunteer to stand in front of the group.

4. Give the volunteer a large sheet of flipchart paper, to hold in front of her. Tell all of the girls that the paper represents a person's feelings and that this activity will demonstrate the impact of *Shredders* on a person's feelings.

5. Ask the girls to listen carefully as you read the following short story aloud. Instruct girls to raise their hands each time they hear a *Shredder* in the story. When they do, a second volunteer from the group should tear a small piece from the flipchart paper that the volunteer is holding in front of her. (Each *Shredder* in the story is indicated by italics, for the facilitator's ease of reference.)

6. By the end of the story, the volunteer should be left with only a fraction of the original paper (do make sure that she has some left to hold). This provides a very visible and memorable image for the participants about the damage that *Shredders* can do.

    ◦ It can make the experience even more memorable to write the words "*Feelings*" or "*Self-esteem*" on the paper prior to reading the story, to emphasize for young girls how these things are "shredded" by the use of insults.

Shredders story

When Gabby woke up in the morning, she was feeling great. She got dressed in her favorite T-shirt and jeans and walked downstairs for breakfast. When she sat down at the table, her mother said, "*Aren't you going to brush that crazy hair of yours?*" When Gabby reached for her hairbrush, her elbow tipped over her sister's glass of milk.

Her sister cried out, *"Way to go, Gabby! Now you ruined my homework!"* Gabby rushed to try to clean up the spill, but in her hurry, she tripped over her little brother's toy car. *"Stupid!"* he cried. *"You just can't do anything right this morning, can you?"* asked Gabby's dad.

Gabby hoped that things would improve once she got to school. She smiled as she walked into her classroom, thinking she was off to a fresh start. She approached her best friend, Maddie, and said, "I'm so excited for the dance tonight!" Maddie looked at Gabby and said, *"You're not planning to wear that, are you?"*

"This is my favorite shirt," said Gabby. "You and I bought it together last week." Maddie gave Gabby a top-to-bottom eye roll and laughed, *"Not my fault!"* Maddie sneered.

The bell rang. Gabby rushed to hang up her coat and get her homework out of her folder. Her teacher said, "Gabby, you should have taken care of all of that before the bell. Now you are late. *You really have to be more responsible, young lady."*

Gabby's face turned bright red. *She looked over and saw Maddie giving Leah "a look."* She knew that look well. It was the look that Maddie usually gave her when they were secretly making fun of someone else.

At lunch, Gabby set her tray down next to Emma. Emma looked up and said, *"Sorry, Gabby. I'm saving that seat for Olivia."* Gabby moved her tray to the other side of the lunch table. When she sat down, Leah said, *"Eeeew. You're having the tacos? Gross! You know that's not real meat, don't you?"* Gabby was too embarrassed to eat her lunch, so she just sat quietly, sipping her chocolate milk until recess.

Outside on the playground, Gabby went to the swings, where she and Maddie met every day at the start of recess. She waited and waited, looking around for what could be keeping her best friend. *She spotted Maddie jumping rope (skipping) with Olivia and Emma on the far end of the blacktop (playground).* Gabby walked over and said, "Can I play too?" Instead of looking at Gabby, *all three girls looked at each other and exchanged smiles.* Emma and Olivia both dropped the jump rope onto the ground. Maddie said, *"Sorry, Gabby. We were just finishing up. We're going to swing now. You can have the rope."*

At the very end of the school day, as all of the kids were packing their bags, Gabby said to Maddie hopefully, "I'll see you tonight at the dance. I can't wait to do our routine together!" Maddie replied, *"Oh! I totally forgot to tell you. I promised Leah I would do the routine with her. Sorry, Gabby. Maybe next time."*

Gabby began to cry.

Processing the activity

- By the end of the story, the original volunteer's paper should be torn to shreds, as a visual reminder of the damage that hurtful words and behaviors can cause. The facilitator should use the following questions to encourage group members to consider the impact of *Shredders*.

  ○ *Gabby said she woke up feeling great. How was Gabby feeling by the end of the day? What caused the change?*

  ○ *How did the* Shredders *from Gabby's family and friends make her feel?*

  ○ *What were some of the hurtful words that you recall?*

  ○ *What behaviors hurt Gabby's feelings?*

  ○ *There is an old saying, "Sticks and stones may break my bones, but words will never hurt me." Since Maddie, Leah, Olivia, and Emma never laid their hands on Gabby to harm her, is it fair to say that Gabby was really hurt?*

  ○ *What could be the effect of Gabby being treated this way day after day?*

  ○ *Have you ever been in a situation where someone's words hurt your feelings?*

- The facilitator should emphasize that despite the old "sticks and stones" adage, words—and even behaviors like knowing glances and smiles—can truly shred a person's feelings and self-esteem. Convey the following points:

  ○ *The words we use really do matter and as members of this group, we will be holding each other accountable for using words in kind, friendship-boosting ways.*

  ○ *In this final activity, we're going to do a "Take 2" and practice building up Gabby's self-esteem, rather than tearing it down.*

- Hand each participant 3–4 blocks. Read Gabby's story, as rewritten below. Tell the girls that this time, whenever they hear Gabby receiving a *"Builder"* (define as a word or behavior that "builds" or boosts a person's self-confidence) they should work together to place a block on top of or next to the block added by the last girl. The object of this activity is to work together to build a structure that represents how tall, strong, and proud *Builders* can make a person feel.

Builders story

When Gabby woke up in the morning, she was feeling great. She got dressed in her favorite T-shirt and jeans and walked downstairs for breakfast. When she sat down at the table, her mother said, *"Good morning, sweetheart. How are you feeling?"* When Gabby reached for her hairbrush, her elbow tipped over her sister's glass of milk. Her sister cried out, "*Oh no! My homework!*" Gabby rushed to help clean up the spill. "*Thanks for helping!*" said her sister. When Gabby went to sit back down, she accidentally tripped over her little brother's toy car. "*Beep, beep!*" he laughed. "It's a bumpy morning for you, Gabby" said her dad, as he *reached out to give her a hug.*

Gabby smiled as she walked into her classroom, looking forward to the day. She approached her best friend, Maddie, and said, "I'm so excited for the dance tonight!" Maddie looked at Gabby and said, "*I know—me too! I hope you're wearing that shirt!*" Gabby smiled, remembering the day last week when Maddie helped her pick it out at the store.

The bell rang. Gabby rushed to hang up her coat and get her homework out of her folder. Her teacher said, "Boys and girls, please make sure you've taken care of all of your responsibilities before the bell rings." Gabby's face turned red as she rushed to get to her seat. She looked over at Maddie, *who gave her a friendly smile.* She knew that look well. It was the look that Maddie usually gave her to *reassure her that mistakes were okay.*

At lunch, Gabby set her tray down next to Emma. Emma looked up and said, "*Hi Gabby. Olivia actually asked me to save that seat for her while she went to the bathroom, but you can sit on this side of me if you want.*" Gabby moved her tray to the other side of Emma. When she sat down, Leah said, "*Yum. Those tacos smell delicious!*" Gabby agreed and enjoyed her lunch with her friends.

Outside on the playground, Gabby went to the swings, where she and Maddie met every day at the start of recess. It *made both girls feel great to know that they could always count on each other.* Usually, the two of them played alone, but today, Maddie suggested they join up with Olivia and Emma to jump rope (skip). The four girls took turns holding the rope and jumping, until the bell rang to signal the end of recess. "*That was fun. Let's do this again tomorrow!*" they agreed.

At the very end of the school day, as all of the kids were packing their bags, Gabby said to Maddie, "I'll see you tonight at the dance. I can't wait to do our routine together!" Maddie replied, "*I know. I'm so excited. See you there!*"

Gabby smiled.

Processing the activity

By the end of this version of the story, the girls should have formed a tall, sturdy structure with the blocks. Ask questions to compare the impact of the different stories, such as:

- *How does Gabby feel at the end of this story, compared to the first version?*

- *What made the difference in her feelings?*

- *How do words change how Gabby feels about herself?*

- *Have you ever been in a situation where* Builders *from a family member, teacher, or friend helped you feel better?*

- *You worked together to build a tall and sturdy structure. How is this structure similar to how Gabby feels in the second story? How is it different from the paper we used in the first story?*

- *How do you want to make your friends and classmates feel?*

- *What can you do on a daily basis to build others up and avoid tearing them down?*

Session conclusion

Summarize the learning from this session and preview next session's agenda:

- *Today, we began to get to know each other as members of the* Real Friendship *group, and we created our own set of ground rules for how to treat one another and have fun together.*

- *Also, because of what we learned from Gabby's stories, we will avoid* Shredders *and practice building our friends up through kind words and behaviors.*

- *Next week, we will be talking about the kinds of values that we look for in real friends.*

Friendship Journal

1. Hand out the *Friendship Journal* (page 33).

2. Let participants know that each week they will have the opportunity to take what they learn in group and apply it to their everyday lives. The *Friendship Journal* provides each participant with a chance to reflect on what is discussed in group, through writing and/or drawing topics.

   ◦ While the *Friendship Journal* is an important extension of the group learning, it is not meant to feel like "homework."

   ◦ Use care when describing the *Journal*, to help participants see it as a tool for deeper learning, rather than a burden or obligation.

   ◦ Do not assign penalties for incomplete journals, but rather be consistent in encouraging girls to take this extra step toward developing strong friendship skills.

   ◦ Use discretion in assigning writing journals, art journals, or whatever self-expression method will work best for each participant.

3. Topic: *This week, write or draw about a time when you helped someone feel better about him or herself, by using* Builders.

4. *There are no right or wrong answers when it comes to journaling. The purpose of this assignment is to increase awareness of the many things that you can do on a daily basis to be a good friend to others.*

Customizing the curriculum

*   Younger children or those with less experience working in small groups may have difficulty thinking of helpful or appropriate group ground rules. The facilitator can provide additional help with this activity for participants who need it. Likewise, a facilitator can allow greater independence with this activity for older or more experienced group participants.

*   The "Gabby" story can be customized for older or younger groups, with details that make the story most relevant and realistic. Older children may enjoy using blocks for both versions of the story. Rather than tearing paper for the *Shredders* story, older kids can use an already assembled tower, from a game such as Jenga®, and take out a block each time an insulting word or phrase is heard. When the tower falls to the ground, kids get a striking illustration of the power of *Shredders*.

*   Older girls may be interested in learning about *Finding Kind*, a documentary film in which young girls and grown women alike share their true stories about growing up and experiencing bullying disguised as friendship. Created by the founders of the Kind Campaign (www.kindcampaign.com), the film was created to use real girls' experiences to find common ground of kindness and mutual respect. Girls should be encouraged to talk to their parents about *Finding Kind* and secure parental permission before researching the film's availability.

*   When describing the *Friendship Journal* topics, allow for participants to express themselves in whatever way best helps them to reflect on the subject matter. Some girls will enjoy the process of keeping a written journal, others may choose to draw, and still others may opt to talk about the subject matter with a family member or trusted adult after the session.

Friendship Journal

This week, write or draw about a time when you helped someone feel better about him or herself, by using *Builders.*

There are no right or wrong answers when it comes to journaling. The purpose of this assignment is to increase awareness of the many things that you can do on a daily basis to be a good friend to others.

✓

Letter to Parents

Dear Parents,

Thank you for allowing your daughter to participate in the *Real Friendship* group. Encouraging meaningful dialogue around the topic of girls' friendships is one of the most important things that supportive adults can do to help young girls navigate the sometimes choppy, and often confusing, waters of peer relationships.

Real Friendship is a structured 12-week curriculum designed to help preserve the exuberant, confident voices of young girls and strengthen their skills to assertively express their thoughts and feelings in ways that respect others, reject bullying behavior, and reflect important values such as dignity, personal responsibility, empathy, cooperation, connectedness, and self-respect. Based on thought-provoking discussions, engaging games, strength-discovering exercises, and confidence-boosting fun, the hands-on activities in the *Real Friendship* group build critical knowledge and teach important friendship survival skills.

After each group session, your daughter will bring home a *Letter to Parents*, written to keep you up-to-date and informed on group activities. The *Letter to Parents* will offer ideas for real-world discussions and at-home conversation starters, to pick up where the girls' group discussions leave off. With messages reinforced both at home and in group, your daughter will be in the best position to experience real learning and lasting skills.

In our opening group session, the girls played a game to get to know each other and learned about how the *Real Friendship* group will work. The girls read two different versions of a story about a character named Gabby to learn the importance of the words they choose to use with one another. In fact, the girls debunked the old "sticks and stones" myth and learned that words really can hurt. Since verbal abuse accounts for 70 percent of reported bullying the girls learned about how to use *Builders* in place of *Shredders* to develop *Real Friendships* with others.

At home, you play a pivotal role in helping your daughter choose her words carefully. More importantly, you play the critical role of teaching her to *choose words* to talk assertively and directly about feelings instead of using socially aggressive behaviors to bully others. Whenever you encourage meaningful dialogue with your daughter, you give her skills for constructive self-expression.

The most effective parents are the ones who actively listen to their daughters. Use the after-group time to engage your daughter in a conversation about friendships. Open-ended questions, such as the ones suggested below, are great ways to get the ball rolling. (Be prepared to listen to any answers that you receive.

It is often surprising how harsh girls' language is, even at young ages, but when your daughter realizes that you will listen without judgment, she is more likely to continue opening up about her life.)

- What kinds of words do kids use to hurt each other?

- What do girls fight about?

- How do you let a friend know when you are feeling angry or upset?

- How do you react if a friend tells you she is angry or upset with you?

- How do girls use technology and social media to hurt each other?

Don't worry about phrasing the questions just right; the specific words you use are not nearly as important as the simple fact that you are initiating and encouraging dialogue with your daughter on a regular and consistent basis. Be sure to get her talking about her life on a daily basis—not just when she is facing a friendship problem—to help her develop comfort and skills for honest self-expression.

In the coming weeks of the *Real Friendship* group, your daughter will be learning practical, real-life skills, including:

- recognizing the red flags of girl bullying

- responding assertively to bullying behavior

- realizing personal strengths

- connecting with healthy friendships

- becoming an ally to others facing bullying

- resolving conflicts directly

- using technology and social media ethically

- making values-based decisions

- reaching out to trustworthy adults.

Each week, your daughter will come home with a *Friendship Journal* topic. You can encourage her to use her journal to record her thoughts and feelings, either by drawing or writing—or both! Keeping a regular journal is a great way for girls to explore and express their inner voices, just as they are practicing skills for out-loud self-expression through group participation and meaningful dialogue with you.

Session 2

Cast Your Vote!
Identifying the Values
of Real Friendship

Session objectives

- To build group trust and cohesion through a *Journal Sharing* activity.

- To discuss the values and behaviors that contribute to *Real Friendship*.

Materials needed

- 15 tokens for each group participant (coins, dried beans, and/or poker chips all work well as tokens)

- 18–20 plastic cups, large enough to hold a few dozen tokens

- flipchart paper and markers

- (optional) wooden craft sticks for selecting small groups.

Before beginning

- Label each plastic cup with a *Friendship Value* from the *Friendship Values* handout (page 42).

- Pre-print the phrase, "*A Real Friend is someone who…*" on flipchart paper.

- Prepare copies of the *Friendship Journal* (page 43) for each participant.

- Prepare copies of the *Letter to Parents* handout (page 44) for each participant to take home.

Welcome back

1. Welcome participants back for their second session of the *Real Friendship* group.

2. Convey that you are eager to get right back into the group interaction and learning about the types of values and behaviors that make for healthy friendships.

Opening activity: Journal Sharing

1. Arrange the participants in a circle, sitting either on chairs or on the floor. Briefly review the activities and discussions from the first session:

   ◦ *Last time we met, we read two versions of a story about a girl named Gabby. Who can tell me about the first version of the story?*

   ◦ *What was different about the second version of Gabby's story?*

   ◦ *This week, did you have any experiences with* Shredders *or* Builders*? Please share.*

   ◦ *Your* Friendship Journal *assignment was to write or draw about a time when you helped someone feel better about him or herself by using* Builders. *Who would like to share their* Journal?

2. In order to encourage openness and active participation at this early stage of the group, each girl who wants to share her Journal should be given the opportunity to do so. Since this is an opening exercise, however, try to keep the total *Journal Sharing* time to no more than ten minutes. Affirm each participant's response, thank them for sharing, allow brief comments from group members, and continue until everyone who wants to share has done so.

3. Assure girls that group members will never be required to share. The more participants open up and talk about their experiences—both the good and the bad—the more everyone will benefit from the group. On the other hand, it is permissible to "pass" on sharing from time to time. Girls should not have to share why they choose to "pass." Allowing girls to make their own decisions about participation builds trust and feelings of safety within the group.

4. Emphasize that the learning that goes on in group is most effective when the girls carry it into their real lives. Journal entries are a great place to start with thinking about and recording their new skills.

Values Voting

The purpose of the *Values Voting* activity is to encourage the girls to think about and discuss the characteristics and behaviors that make for *Real Friendship*. The values identified in this activity will be referred to several times throughout the rest of the group sessions.

1. Ask for volunteers to define the term "value" in their own words.

    ◦   Affirm that "value" can mean monetary worth, but it also has to do with the types of beliefs and behaviors that are important to a person.

2. Ask for volunteers to list 2–3 examples of *Friendship Values*, or behaviors that are important in a friendship. The facilitator may suggest examples from the *Friendship Values* handout (page 42). It may help to start with a phrase such as:

    ◦   *"A Real Friend is someone who…"*

    ◦   *"I like to spend time with friends who…"*

    Challenge participants to complete the sentence with a *Friendship Value* statement.

3. Tell the girls that they are going to participate in an activity to learn about what group members value most in real friends.

4. Give each girl 15 tokens. Show the girls that around the room, there are several different plastic cups, each labeled with a specific *Friendship Value*. Explain the rules as follows:

    ◦   *You are each going to "cast your votes" for the* Friendship Values *that you believe are most important. You will vote by putting your tokens into the cups that represent each value.*

    ◦   *You can divide your tokens any way you want. For example, you can put all 15 tokens in a single cup if there is one* Friendship Value *you think is the most important of all. Or, you can put one token into each of 15 different cups, if you feel that the values are of equal importance.*

    ◦   *The only rule is that you have five minutes to distribute all of your tokens.*

Processing the activity

1. It may be helpful to write the sentence starter, "*A Real Friend is someone who…*" on a piece of flipchart paper, for all the girls to see.

2. After five minutes, bring the large group back together. Use the following questions to guide a large group discussion about the values group members selected:

    ○   *What values did you vote for?*

    ○   *Why are those values important when it comes to making and keeping friendships?*

3. The facilitator should ask for volunteers to count the tokens in each *Friendship Values* cup. Use flipchart paper to tally the group results.

    ○   *Which values received the highest number of tokens?*

    ○   *What does it mean to you that these values are shared by so many group members?*

    ○   *Were there any* Friendship Values *that received no votes? Why do you think that is?* (It may be necessary for the facilitator to clarify that some of the cups are labeled with undesirable values, to illustrate the point that some behaviors are hurtful to friendship.)

    ○   *Are there any different* Friendship Values *you would have voted for if they had been available? What are they?*

    ○   *What are some behaviors you use to show someone that you are a good friend?*

4. Wrap up the discussion by thanking the girls for their active participation in *Values Voting*. In your own words, convey the following:

    ○   *In real life, we can't just cast a vote for a perfect friendship. In fact, there is no such thing as a perfect person or a perfect friend. On the other hand, when you know ahead of time the friendship qualities you value, it can help you make smart choices when it comes to making friends and being a good friend to others.*

    ○   *Our group is off to a great start, thanks to your willingness to talk about the qualities that you value in friendship.*

    ○   *As our sessions go on, we will be talking about these same values again and again as we learn about creating healthy friendships and feeling good about ourselves.*

Session conclusion

- *Today, we talked about the values that each of us look for in our friends. We know that this group is a safe place where girls will learn and practice* Friendship Values.

- *Next week, we will talk about a type of behavior that goes against the* Friendship Values *we voted on today and learn two rules for stopping that behavior before it can damage friendships.*

Friendship Journal

1. Hand out the *Friendship Journal* (page 43).

2. Topic: *What is a* Friendship Value *that is important to you? Write or draw about a time when you acted out that value with a friend.*

3. Remind girls that there are no right or wrong answers when it comes to journaling. The purpose of this activity is to encourage girls to think about how they live *Friendship Values* in their everyday lives.

Customizing the curriculum

- Younger girls may be less familiar with the concept of "values" and need more guidance from the facilitator in brainstorming and defining *Friendship Values*. Consider eliminating the negative *Friendship Values* (e.g. *gets mad a lot, leaves me out*) as these may confuse younger girls and cause them to believe that these are desirable behaviors.

- Older group participants may benefit from working in pairs to cast their *Values Votes*. Use the *Craft Stick Method* (see page 21) to assign partners and encourage girls to discuss each value before determining their joint votes.

- The facilitator can add to or change the wording of specific values, in order to make the activity most relevant and age-appropriate.

✓

Activity: Friendship Values

Facilitator notes

Print the Friendship Values *listed below as labels for plastic cups for the* Values Voting *activity. The facilitator can add to or change the wording of specific values, in order to make the activity most relevant and age-appropriate.*

A Real Friend is someone who…

- uses kind words
- takes turns and cooperates
- shares
- uses words to tell me how she feels
- helps me when I need it
- compliments me
- includes me
- is always there for me
- understands how I feel
- cares about my opinions and feelings
- stands up for me
- is fun to be with
- has a lot in common with me
- talks behind my back
- makes fun of other people
- gets other girls to gang up on me
- gets mad a lot
- bosses me around.

✓

Friendship Journal

What is a *Friendship Value* that is important to you? Write or draw about a time when you acted out that value with a friend.

Remember: There are no right or wrong answers when it comes to journaling!

Letter to Parents

Dear Parents,

Today, in the *Real Friendship* group, your daughter exercised her right to vote! Through a brainstorming session and hands-on *Values Voting* activity, the girls were encouraged to discuss the characteristics and behaviors that make for *Real Friendship*. Ask your daughter to tell you about the *Friendship Values* that she and her groupmates rated most highly.

It might even be fun to host your own at-home voting booth; consider gathering family members in a discussion about important *Friendship Values* such as:

- being there for a friend in need

- showing kindness

- understanding how a friend feels

- taking turns

- caring about a friend's opinions and feelings

- cooperating

- standing up for a friend

- sharing

- having a lot in common

- using words to express thoughts and feelings

- giving compliments to a friend

- helping a friend.

The values identified today in the *Real Friendship* group will be referenced throughout the rest of the group sessions, as girls are reminded of their responsibility to make healthy choices when it comes to friendships.

You are your daughter's most powerful and influential role model when it comes to encouraging her to make values-based decisions. Take advantage of "teachable moments" to talk with your daughter about how you live your values through your behaviors and interactions with others.

Silent Whispers
Two Rules for Stopping Gossip

Session objectives

- To understand the process of rumor-spreading and gossip.
- To identify these behaviors as hurtful to *Real Friendship*.
- To learn and practice two strategies for stopping rumors and gossip.

Materials needed

- wooden craft sticks for selecting small groups
- flipchart paper and markers.

Before beginning

- Prepare the *Stopping Rumors and Gossip* flipchart paper with the following two rules pre-printed:

  i. *"Refuse to whisper down the alley."*

  ii. *"Tell the person to stop spreading rumors and gossip."*

- Prepare copies of the *Friendship Journal* (page 51) for each participant.
- Prepare copies of the *Letter to Parents* handout (page 52) for each participant to take home.

Welcome back

1.   Welcome participants back for their third session of the *Real Friendship* group.

2.   Review the previous session:

     ◦   *Last week, you each cast your votes for the* Friendship Values *that are most important to you. As a group, we determined that values such as (list three top values from the tally sheet) are important to any* Real Friendship.

     ◦   *Since we last met, have you had any chances to see* Real Friendship Values *in action? Please share.*

3.   Preview this week's agenda:

     ◦   *This week, we are going learn about a behavior that goes against the values of* Real Friendship.

     ◦   *We will also learn specific strategies for how to stop this behavior and stand up for* Real Friendship Values.

Opening activity: Whisper Down the Alley

1.   Tell the girls that the group is going to play a round of the game *Whisper Down the Alley.* The same children's game may be better known to some as *Telephone* or *Operator.* While many girls may be familiar with this popular group game, a quick rules review will be helpful:

     ◦   *I will whisper a sentence into the ear of the girl next to me. She will whisper the words she hears into the ear of the next girl in the circle, and so on, until the message is passed to all of the girls.*

     ◦   *The only rules are that you cannot ask the person to repeat what they whisper to you and you must repeat back exactly what you hear—or think you hear—to the next person.*

     ◦   *The final girl in the circle should announce the phrase aloud to the group. The facilitator who started the original sentence will verify if the message was transmitted correctly or incorrectly.*

2.   The facilitator should initiate the first round of play, using the following sentence:

     ◦   *I heard that Jenny likes Rachel but Rachel is best friends with Cassie and Cassie doesn't like Jenny (because Jenny likes Beth who is in a big fight with Cassie).*

- ○ The bracketed part of the sentence may be added/eliminated, depending on the age level of the participants. While the sentence is intended to have a lot of detail, the first half may be sufficient for younger groups.

3. Per the rules, resist any requests for repeating the sentence, but rather let it travel around the circle completely. Chances are excellent that some of the details will become distorted along the way. At the end of the game play, ask the girls to reflect on the distortions:

- ○ *Did* [name of final girl in the circle] *say the same message that I started?*

- ○ *How were the messages different?*

- ○ *Why did the message change as it was passed among the group members?*

- ○ *Does anyone know another word for a message that spreads between kids, but is usually whispered, written about, or "spoken behind people's backs?" This kind of message often starts with words like, "I heard..." or "Did you hear..."*

4. Encourage girls to identify the words "rumor" and/or "gossip."

- ○ *How is the game* Whisper Down the Alley *like real life gossip and rumor-spreading?*

- ○ *Notice how the names and details changed when the sentence was being passed around. In real-life gossip, can kids hurt one another by spreading incorrect messages and unkind information? How can you help stop this from happening?*

- ○ *Why is it important to express your thoughts and feelings out loud and directly to a person, rather than whispering about them to someone else?*

- ○ *What can you do when someone you know is spreading a rumor?*

5. Summarize the discussion with a statement about how rumors and gossip are a bad idea when it comes to building healthy friendships.

Stopping Rumors and Gossip

1. Encourage participants to be the kind of girl who stops rumors, rather than spreading them:

- ○ *When you stop rumors, you show that you are the kind of girl who lives by* Real Friendship Values. *Stopping rumors is a powerful friendship move and can be done in two simple steps.*

2. Show girls the *Stopping Rumors* and *Gossip* flipchart paper with the following two rules pre-printed:

     i. *"Refuse to whisper down the alley."* (In other words, refuse to repeat gossip to others.)

     ii. *"Tell the person to stop spreading rumors and gossip."*

3. It is helpful to coach girls about how to tell a person to stop spreading rumors and gossip. In the next two sessions, we will be talking in detail about assertive phrasing, but for the purposes of this activity, it is helpful to encourage the following:

   ◦ *Look the rumor-starter in the eye and use a strong (but not raised) voice to say, "That sounds like a rumor. You should talk with* [name of person rumor is about] *and not spread that to anyone else."*

4. It may be helpful to write the phrasing above on flipchart paper, so that the girls can refer to it in the upcoming exercise.

5. Tell the girls that they are going to practice using the two steps for stopping rumors and gossip.

6. Using the *Craft Stick Method* (see page 21), arrange girls into pairs (or groups of three, as needed). Tell the girls that they will take turns being a rumor-starter and a rumor-stopper. Explain:

   ◦ *The first girl will turn to the girl on her right and say, "I heard that* [choose any girl's name, avoiding the name of any girl in the group]*…"*

   ◦ *After just those first four words, the second girl should look the first girl in the eye and say in a firm voice, "That sounds like a rumor. You should talk with* [name of person rumor is about] *and not spread that to anyone else."*

7. After the first round, the girls should switch roles, so that each girl has the opportunity to practice saying the words to stop gossip in its tracks.

8. Give each girl the chance to play both roles, then bring the large group back together for a wrap-up discussion:

   ◦ *How did it feel to stop the rumor?*

   ◦ *Why is it important to stop rumors and gossip?*

   ◦ *How do rumors and gossip hurt friendships? How do they hurt individuals?*

   ◦ *Has anyone ever told a rumor about you? How did it make you feel?*

○ *Have you ever stopped a rumor that someone else started? How did that make you feel?*

9. Affirm each response and encourage discussion that underscores the idea that rumors and gossip are harmful to friendship and to a girl's self-esteem and that girls have the power to stop these behaviors.

Session conclusion

• Emphasize that understanding the harmful effects of rumors and learning skills for stopping them is an important first step in forming *Real Friendships*.

• Preview that in the next session, the girls are going to talk about other behaviors that go against *Friendship Values* and need to be stopped in their tracks.

Friendship Journal

1. Hand out the *Friendship Journal* (page 51).

2. Topic: *This week, notice the kinds of things you hear girls saying about each other. Do you hear more kind phrases or unkind ones? Record some of the examples that you hear. If gossip is told to you directly, practice stopping the gossip. Use the Journal to share how you are able to live your* Friendship Values *and stop behaviors that go against them.*

3. Remind girls that there are no right or wrong answers when it comes to journaling. The purpose of this activity is to increase girls' awareness of their role in stopping gossip and rumor-spreading.

Customizing the curriculum

• In the game *Whisper Down the Alley*, add detail and complexity to the whispered phrases used with older group participants. Tailor follow-up discussion questions to the level of participants and to the depth of their real-world experiences.

- Older participants are likely to have real-life examples of rumors that have been started and spread. Allow girls to share so that the group experience becomes most relevant, but not to the extent that actual girls and identifiable incidents are exposed. When situations become too specific, confidentiality is risked and group members will feel less safe in sharing personal information.

- If time permits, allow volunteers to present their rumor-stopping role play in front of the large group.

Friendship Journal

This week, notice the kinds of things you hear girls saying about each other. Do you hear more kind phrases or unkind ones? Record some of the examples that you hear. If gossip is told to you directly, practice stopping the gossip. Use the journal to share how you are able to live your *Friendship Values* and stop behaviors that go against them.

Letter to Parents

Dear Parents,

Today, in the *Real Friendship* group, your daughter played *Whisper Down the Alley* to learn about how rumors and gossip are a bad idea when it comes to building healthy friendships. This classic game took on a whole new meaning for the girls, as they experienced first-hand how words can be twisted and meanings can change drastically when they are passed from one girl to another.

Since one of the priorities of the *Real Friendship* group is to encourage girls to use their authentic, assertive voices, participants were asked to consider:

> *Why is it important to express your thoughts and feelings out loud and directly to a person, rather than whispering about them to someone else?*

This is a great discussion point for follow-up at home. Young girls often face enormous social pressure to be "good" at all costs, a standard that squashes honest self-expression and drives many girls to mask the way they convey angry feelings, lest they be looked upon as "bad" girls. *How to Be Angry: An Assertive Anger Expression Group Guide for Kids and Teens* (Whitson 2011) provides at-home discussion ideas and activities for teaching girls how to express anger—and other authentic emotions—in assertive, relationship-enhancing ways. When girls learn to communicate assertively, they live up to the *Friendship Values* discussed last week.

Ask your daughter to tell you the two specific rules she learned for stopping rumors and gossip. Use role play to give your daughter the opportunity to practice these rules. With repetition, these *Real Friendship* skills can become second nature to young girls and provide them with a lifelong foundation for healthy peer relationships.

The Red Flags of Girl Bullying
When Friendship Is Used as a Weapon

Session objectives

- To understand common behaviors girls use to hurt others.
- To establish a definition of "bullying."
- To develop initial strategies to ban bullying behaviors.

Materials needed

- wooden craft sticks for selecting small groups
- flipchart paper and markers
- index cards.

Before beginning

- Prepare scenarios from the *Behaviours that Are Hurtful to Friendship* handout (page 63) for each small group.
- Prepare index cards from the *Bully Bans* and *Using Bully Bans* handouts (pages 64 and 65).
- Prepare copies of the *Friendship Journal* (page 66) for each participant.
- Prepare copies of the *Letter to Parents* handout (page 67) for each participant to take home.

Welcome back

1. Welcome the girls back for the fourth group session.

2. Review the learning from last week:

   ° *Who remembers the game we played at the beginning of our last meeting?* (Whisper Down the Alley.)

   ° *In* Whisper Down the Alley, *we saw first-hand how rumors and gossip can be hurtful to friendship and to how girls feel about themselves. What were the two rules we practiced for* Stopping Rumors and Gossip?

      i. Refuse to repeat rumors and gossip.

      ii. Tell the person to stop spreading rumors and gossip.

   ° *Did anyone have a chance to practice this week? Without naming names or using details that would embarrass someone, tell the group about the situation.*

3. Preview the agenda for this week:

   ° *Today, we are going to talk about other behaviors, along with rumor-spreading and gossip, that are hurtful to friendship and damaging to how girls feel about themselves. We are also going to practice new ways of stopping those behaviors.*

   ° *First, let's play a game that shows how people express themselves without using words.*

Opening activity: Friendship Charades

1. To introduce the idea of how girls communicate angry feelings without ever having to talk about them directly, begin with a brief game of charades.

2. Ask for a volunteer. Whisper in her ear a simple action phrase (e.g. *open the door, turn on the light, write a note,* etc.). Instruct her to silently act out the phrase in front of the group.

3. Group members should try to guess what the volunteer is acting out. When the phrase is guessed correctly, allow another volunteer to take a turn or move on to process the activity (suggested questions on page 55).

4. Allow 2–3 volunteers the opportunity to act out an activity. It may be helpful to use the *Craft Stick Method* to select volunteers for this activity (see page 21), since it is likely that many girls will want the opportunity to act out an activity. Thank all girls for their eagerness to participate and assure them that the rest of the session will allow each girl the opportunity to act and role play.

5. Use the following questions to process *Friendship Charades*:

   ◦ *In this game, how did each volunteer communicate meaning?* (Using her body, facial expressions, gestures, etc.)

   ◦ *Even though she was not allowed to use words, were you able to understand her?*

   ◦ *Sometimes, when girls are angry with a friend, they choose not to use words to express their feelings. Instead, they express their anger through behaviors. Like in our game of charades, the meaning behind their behaviors is usually pretty obvious.*

   ◦ *Today, we are going to talk about some of the most common ways that girls show their feelings through hurtful behaviors.*

   ◦ *We are also going to learn about how important it is for girls to use their voices and their words to express feelings, rather than relying on hurtful, unspoken behaviors.*

Introduction to girl bullying: How NOT to Be a Friend

1. Using the *Craft Stick Method*, divide girls into pairs or groups of three to read 1–2 scenarios from the *How NOT to be a Friend* handout (page 61). Give each group of girls different selections of scenarios.

2. Assign each small group to identify the behavior(s) in the scenario(s) that goes against *Friendship Values*. Depending on the age of the group members, it may be helpful for a facilitator to check in with each small group as they are working, to ensure their comprehension of the scenario and ability to identify the friendship-damaging behavior(s).

3. After each group has finished (no more than five minutes), invite the small groups to come back together. One by one, call on each small group to read their scenario aloud (with assistance, if necessary) and identify the behavior that is hurtful to friendship.

4. Using flipchart paper and markers, record the girls' responses. It is helpful to write, *"Behaviors that Are Hurtful to Friendship"* at the top of the flipchart paper, to reinforce the purpose of the activity and discussion. Tie this activity in to the story about Gabby from Session 1 and remind the girls that these types of behaviours "shred" a person's feelings and self-esteem.

5. After each group has taken their turn, ask the girls if they can think of other behaviors and incidents from their real lives that hurt people's feelings and damage friendships. Remind girls that to protect confidentiality and guard against rumor-spreading, real names should not be used.

6. Because of the young age of many participants, some girls may have difficulty generating ideas, especially at the beginning. This is a great time for the facilitator to encourage examples based on knowledge of the kinds of issues and situations common to the particular group. See the sample *Behaviors that Are Hurtful to Friendship* list (page 63).

7. When the list seems complete, it is time to be very direct with the girls about the nature of the behaviors they have just identified and to begin defining them under the realm of bullying. Use the following as a guide:

   ◦ *We just created a list called* Behaviors that Are Hurtful to Friendship. *There is one word that can be used to describe all of the behaviors we just discussed. Can anyone guess what that word is?*

8. The facilitator can give hints and clues (e.g. *"It is a word that begins with the letter B,"* or *"Some people think of a strong boy who uses his fists when they hear this word,"* etc.) as necessary. The important thing is that the word "Bully" is identified, spoken aloud and used clearly as a defining term.

   ◦ *Sometimes, when people hear the word "bullying," their first thought is of a bigger kid hitting, kicking, or threatening a smaller kid. In truth, bullying also includes exactly the kinds of behaviors we just listed.*

   ◦ *When girls spread rumors, gossip, leave each other out, ignore one another, give mean looks, gang up on each other, etc. (the facilitator can add other specifics from the list), these behaviors can be just as painful as being punched.*

   ◦ *In fact, these kinds of behaviors, disguised as friendship, are often even more damaging in the long term to friendships and how a girl feels about herself.*

   ◦ *Keep in mind that when these kinds of behaviors are acted out once, they might mean that the person is in a bad mood or having a rough day. On the other hand, when you notice that a "friend" uses these behaviors day after day, it is important for you to be able to recognize and understand them as bullying.*

9. Under the heading, *Behaviors that Are Hurtful to Friendship*, the facilitator should add the word, "*Bullying.*" Continue by conveying the following:

   ○ *We have all had experiences with hurtful friendship behaviors and bullying. Perhaps we've even carried out a few of the behaviors on the list ourselves. That's understandable. We've all been there and we've all done things we wish we could take back.*

   ○ *Sometimes, you may even feel like this is how you are "supposed" to behave, since we see hurtful friendship behaviors on TV, in movies, and all around us.*

   ○ *From this point forward, however, let's agree to make a change.*

   ○ *Today, we are defining these behaviors as bullying and as a violation of the* Friendship Values *we voted on. As a group, let's agree to "ban" this type of behavior.* (The facilitator should add the word "*Ban*" before the word "*Bullying*" on the flipchart.)

   ○ *From this point forward, we will hold each other accountable for treating each other according to* Friendship Values *and refusing to participate in these kinds of bullying behaviors.*

Bully Bans

- To round out this session's discussion about bullying behaviors, it is important for girls to learn and practice initial strategies for "banning bullying."

- Group members will establish a set of assertive phrases—or *Bully Bans*—that they can use anytime they notice that a bullying behavior is taking place. Learning about assertive phrasing now will assist girls during the next session when they put together four rules for *STANding up to Girl Bullying.*

- The facilitator should define *Bully Bans* as short, to-the-point statements that let others know that you will not participate in their bullying, nor will you be bullied.

- It is important to remind girls that *Bully Bans* do not put down or attack the bully, which is never a good idea. Likewise, *Bully Bans* are not effective when said through tears or a whining voice. (More detail on using body language and tone of voice will be provided next session.) *Bully Bans* are brief, assertive statements used to stand up to bullies and stop bullying behavior.

- It is helpful for the facilitator to role model an example of an effective *Bully Ban*, spoken in an assertive tone of voice. Ask for a volunteer to stand in front of you in the room. Hand her a card (from the *Using Bully Bans* handout, page 65) with the phrase, "*I'm not going to be your friend anymore if you play with Bella.*" Instruct her to say the phrase to you aloud. Respond back with an assertive *Bully Ban* such as, "*I don't like to be treated that way.*"

- Challenge participants to think of their own *Bully Bans* and share them with the group. Record effective assertive phrases on a flipchart. Help reformulate suggestions from girls that might err on the side of aggression or passivity. The phrases that are written on the flipchart will probably be interpreted as "good" by the girls, so take care to edit responses before recording them. For your reference, a sample list of *Bully Bans* is provided on page 64. The facilitator can add these sample phrases to supplement the list developed by the girls. Aim to have at least 7–10 options for assertive *Bully Bans* on a completed list.

Using Bully Bans

1. Tell the girls that the final activity of the session will be to practice using *Bully Bans*. Have the girls return to the same small groups they formed earlier. Hand each girl 1–2 pre-printed index cards from the *Using Bully Bans* handout (page 65). In each group, one girl should play the role of a bully, using the phrase from their index card. A second girl should select a phrase from the *Bully Bans* list (page 64) and practice using it as an assertive response to the bully.

2. Encourage the girls to take turns being the bully and the responder within their small groups. Ideally, each girl should get at least two opportunities to practice using *Bully Bans*. It is helpful for a facilitator to be available to observe each role play and coach the girls on their tone of voice and body language as they practice using *Bully Bans*, as this skill poses a challenge to many young girls.

3. After each girl has had the opportunity to practice using *Bully Bans*, the facilitator should wrap up the activity with a brief discussion:

   ○ *Why are* Bully Bans *important?*

   ○ *How did it make you feel to stand up for yourself, using a* Bully Ban*?*

   ○ *How did the bully respond?*

   ○ *How can using* Bully Bans *make a difference in your friendships?*

Session conclusion

- Affirm the girls for their active participation and thoughtful responses:

    ○ *Most of us think that friendship should be all about fun and feeling good about ourselves when we are with our friends. And we are right!*

    ○ *Whenever we realize that friendship is being misused to hurt one another, it's time for us to step up and stop the behavior, as best as we can.*

    ○ *Bullying is a lot like the charades game we played. Bullies are afraid to use their voices to express their feelings, so they act out their anger through mean behaviors. It is our job to use our voices, rather than unkind, indirect behaviors, to stand up to bullying.*

    ○ *Next week, we will talk even more about banning bullying and learn four rules for standing up to the kinds of behaviors we have talked about today.*

Friendship Journal

1. Hand out the *Friendship Journal* (page 66).

2. Topic: *This week, fold your Journal page in half. On the left side, share a time when you experienced bullying by a friend. On the right side, share a time when a friend treated you with* Real Friendship Values *that helped you to feel good about yourself.*

3. Remind girls that there are no right or wrong answers when it comes to journaling. The purpose of this assignment is to increase awareness about friendship and the types of values and behaviors that girls are encouraged to look for in a healthy friendship.

Customizing the curriculum

- This section is very dense with activity and information. For younger participants or those who need more time to process each element, it may be helpful to divide this part of the curriculum into two separate sessions.

    ○ If that option is selected, the *Friendship Charades* and *How NOT to Be a Friend* activities may be the focus of a first session, while the *Bully Bans* activity can stand on its own as a follow-up meeting.

○ If the sessions are split, *Friendship Charades* may be played a second time, as this game is often very popular with kids. Also, allow for *Friendship Journal* sharing time and expanded role play of *Bully Bans* during the second meeting.

- The facilitator should determine the relevance of each *How NOT to Be a Friend* scenario prior to the activity. For example, scenarios 11–12 involve the use of cell phones and the internet. For groups of younger girls who may not yet have access to these kinds of technology, these scenarios can be omitted and/or replaced with scenarios most relevant to the girls' everyday experiences.

Activity: How NOT to Be a Friend

Facilitator notes

Cut out each individual scenario below and distribute to pairs or small groups. As necessary, assist girls to read the scenarios and identify the behaviors that may be hurtful to a friendship.

Scenario 1

You raise your hand to answer a math problem, but say the incorrect number. Across the room, Emily laughs and looks at Abby, who laughs and rolls her eyes. You feel embarrassed and stupid.

Scenario 2

You have been best friends with Jasmine since kindergarten (nursery school). This year, you have also become friends with Carly. Yesterday, Jasmine told you that she is not going to talk to Carly anymore and that she doesn't want you to either.

Scenario 3

Tess is having a birthday party. She invited all of the girls in the class, except for you and Bridget. At lunch, all of the girls are whispering about the party in front of you. You are feeling unliked and left out.

Scenario 4

Lisa has been teasing Rachel and calling her "stupid" everyday at recess, when your teacher can't hear her. Today, Lisa tells you to tell everyone on the playground that Rachel doesn't know how to read.

Scenario 5

The school dance is coming up in five days. Lily and Morgan tell you that if you try to dance with them, they will run away. When you start to get upset, Lily says, "It was just a joke. You don't have to be so sensitive about everything!"

Scenario 6

Every day at lunch, you sit with your friends Megan, Molly, and Taylor. Today, when you begin to sit down, they look at you and say, "Sorry, this seat is saved for Liza," then begin to laugh.

Scenario 7

You wear a brand new pair of jeans to school. Brandi looks at you and says loudly to Shannon, "Look who is wearing baby clothes to school again."

Scenario 8

The gym teacher assigns two captains to pick teams for soccer. You are the last girl to be picked. As you walk toward your team, you hear Paige complain, "Why do we always get stuck with her?"

Scenario 9

Alexa is your best friend in your class. Grace lives next door to you and has been your best friend since you were both four. At recess, Alexa says, "I won't be your friend anymore if you play with Grace."

Scenario 10

You and your best friend Zoe had an argument during recess (breaktime). Later, while standing in line to go to the bathroom, Leah walks up to you and tells you that you really shouldn't have been so mean to Zoe. Kylie glares at you from over Leah's shoulder. It is obvious that Zoe has told several of the girls in the class about your argument and now they are all mad at you.

Scenario 11

Four girls are at a sleepover party. The girls begin to gossip about Lanie, a girl from their class who was not invited to the party. Madison takes out the cell phone her mother lent her for an emergency and sends a mean text message about Lanie to the rest of the girls in their class.

Scenario 12

Gwen and Carrie are partners in computer class. When they finish their assignment, Gwen has the idea to start a rumor about Wendy on Facebook. By the end of class, she has posted the comment to more than half of the class.

Handout: Behaviors that Are Hurtful to Friendship

Facilitator notes

This list can be used to supplement participant brainstorming during the Introduction to Girl Bullying: How NOT to Be a Friend *discussion.*

1. Excluding girls from parties and play dates.

2. Talking about parties and play dates in front of girls who are not invited.

3. Laughing and making fun of girls.

4. Using *Shredders*, such as teasing and calling girls names.

5. Giving girls the "silent treatment."

6. Threatening to take away friendship ("*I won't be your friend anymore if…*").

7. Encouraging others to "gang up" on a girl you are angry with.

8. Spreading rumors and starting gossip about a girl.

9. Saying mean things about a girl's clothing or appearance.

10. Using special toys and treats to include some kids and make others feel left out.

11. "Forgetting" to save a seat for a friend or leaving a girl out by "saving a seat" for someone else.

12. Saying something mean and then following it with "just joking" to try to avoid blame.

13. Using cell phones and/or the internet to gossip, start rumors, or say mean things to a girl.

Handout: Bully Bans

Facilitator notes

This list can be used to supplement participant brainstorming during the Bully Bans *activity.*

1. "That hurts our friendship."

2. "Not cool!"

3. "That sounds like a rumor to me."

4. "Knock it off."

5. "Friends don't treat each other that way."

6. "I need a friend that will treat me kindly."

7. "That's no way to treat a friend."

8. "Cut it out."

9. "Stop it."

10. "Don't be mean to me."

11. "I don't want to be treated that way."

12. "I like the way I look."

13. "That was not funny."

14. "I don't like what you did/said."

15. "I don't like how you are treating me."

16. "I can take a joke, but what you said was not funny—it was mean."

17. "Friends don't do that to friends."

18. "That's bullying."

Activity: Using Bully Bans

Facilitator notes

Give each girl 1–2 index cards pre-printed with a "Shredder" bullying phrase from the list below. The girl should read the phrase aloud, then allow her partner to respond with an assertive Bully Ban.

I'm not going to be your friend anymore if you play with Bella.	Why do you always wear dresses to school? Dresses are for babies.
You can't sit here. This seat is saved for someone else.	You can't play with us today. We're playing something that's just for girls who are in our club.
Eeew. You always bring the grossest foods for lunch. Don't sit near me.	I was just joking. I don't know why you are getting so upset.

✓

Friendship Journal

This week, fold your Journal page in half. On the left side, share a time when you experienced bullying by a friend. On the right side, share a time when a friend treated you with *Real Friendship Values* that helped you to feel good about yourself.

Letter to Parents

Dear Parents,

In the culture of young girls, social norms dictate that anger cannot be voiced directly, so this powerful emotion is concealed behind an angry smile (see *The Angry Smile*, by Long, Long and Whitson 2009) and conflict is waged in ruthlessly passive aggressive ways. The *Real Friendships* curriculum takes aim at this damaging cultural constraint. It encourages girls to find their voice when it comes to talking about anger and conflict and to gain confidence for speaking about them assertively, rather than acting out through hurtful behaviors.

Today, in the *Real Friendship* group, your daughter learned some of the most important and eye-opening lessons that the group has to offer. In particular, the girls used common, real-world scenarios to identify behaviors that are hurtful to friendship and then defined these behaviors as examples of Bullying. The group revisited lessons from previous weeks to identify behaviors like repeated use of "*Shredders,*" and spreading rumors as examples of Bullying. They also added everyday weapons of friendship, such as exclusion, alliance-building, and the dreaded use of the silent treatment to their list of *Behaviors that Are Hurtful to Friendship*. Ask your daughter to share with you specific examples and scenarios that were discussed in the group.

This session is all about violating cultural norms and talking about girl bullying behaviors directly, rather than allowing them to fester and grow behind the scenes. Moreover, the *Real Friendships* curriculum aims to assure young girls that it is okay to speak out against bullying whenever they become aware that it is taking place. To that end, today your daughter learned how to use *Bully Bans*. *Bully Bans* are short, to-the-point statements that let others know that she will not participate in their bullying, nor will she be bullied. Ask her to share examples of the *Bully Bans* that were brainstormed during group. Use role play to allow her the opportunity to practice this assertive skill at home.

There are many everyday ways that you can help your daughter recognize the red flags of *Girl Bullying* and encourage her to respond to it assertively, including:

- talking about friendship dilemmas

- teaching her skills to address conflict directly

- giving her opportunities to have a voice in meaningful family matters

- role modeling assertive behavior

- accepting her angry feelings in an empathic way.

Doing Hand STANds
Four Rules for STANding up to Girl Bullying

Session objectives

- To learn four rules for *STANding up to Bullying*.
- To create an original slogan about *STANDing up to Bullying*.

Materials needed

- flipchart paper and markers
- unlined paper for each participant
- pencils, crayons, and markers for each participant.

Before beginning

- Use flipchart paper to pre-print *"The Four Rules for STANding up to Bullying,"* as follows:
  - **S**how Strength
  - **T**ell an Adult
  - **A**ssert Yourself
  - **N**ow!
- Using flipchart paper, pre-print a *Hand STANd* (see page 78), with an original slogan and examples.
- Prepare copies of the *Friendship Journal* (page 79) for each participant.

- Prepare copies of the *Letter to Parents* handout (page 80) for each participant to take home.

Welcome back

1. Welcome girls to the fifth group session.

2. Review last week's session on *Bullying and Bully Bans:*

   ○ *The last time we met as a group, we talked about behaviors that are hurtful to girls and to their friendships. We gave those kinds of behaviors a name. Who remembers what we called them?* (Bullying.)

   ○ *We also came up with a list of* Bully Bans. Bully Bans *are short, to-the-point statements that let others know that you will not participate in their bullying, nor will you be bullied. What were some of the* Bully Ban *statements we came up with?* (Refer to the flipcharted list from last session or the *Bully Bans* handout on page 64.)

   ○ *Did anyone have an occasion to witness bullying or use a* Bully Ban *this week?* (Remind girls not to use names or information that would identify a specific person.)

3. Preview this week's agenda:

   ○ *Today, we are going to talk about four rules for* STANding up to Bullying *behavior.*

   ○ *Each of you will be challenged to come up with a personal anti-bullying slogan.*

   ○ *First, we are going to start with a brief activity to talk about what* not *to do when it comes to standing up to bullying.*

Opening activity: Wrong Way

1. Arrange the girls in a sitting circle. Explain the activity as follows:

   ○ *When someone uses bully behaviors with you, a natural reaction is for you to feel sad, mad, scared, or even confused. Sometimes, though, if we act on our feelings right away, we end up making the situation worse instead of better.*

   ○ *Today in group, we are going to learn four basic rules for standing up to bullying, but before we do, let's take turns thinking about some of the not-so-helpful ways that people react to bullies.*

○ *We will go around the circle and each of you will have the chance to share one "wrong way" to handle bullying. If another group member says your answer before it is your turn, it's okay for you to repeat the same thing; this emphasizes how common that response can be.*

2. The facilitator should go first to role model the activity. Common "wrong ways" to respond to bullying usually fall under the categories of passive (P), aggressive (AG), and passive aggressive (PA) behaviors. Older participants may benefit from classifying the responses as such. Younger ones do not need to make these distinctions. For all ages, it is helpful to encourage clear examples of unhelpful responses, such as the following:

   ○ ignoring the person even after she bullies you repeatedly (P)

   ○ complimenting the bully and trying to be her friend right after she bullies you (P)

   ○ keeping the bullying a secret (P)

   ○ calling the bully names (AG)

   ○ yelling at the bully (AG)

   ○ hitting or kicking the bully (AG)

   ○ giving the bully the silent treatment (PA)

   ○ spreading rumors about the bully (PA).

3. After each girl has had the opportunity to share an answer, summarize this opening activity:

   ○ *These reactions you have shared are normal and natural, but keep in mind that they are also unhelpful when it comes to coping with bullying.*

   ○ *Often, they even make a bullying situation worse.*

   ○ *To show you how to make a bullying situation better, we are going to learn four rules for effectively standing up to bullies.*

The Four Rules for STANding up to Bullying

1. *When bullying is disguised as friendship, it often takes us by surprise. It is helpful to memorize the steps for STANding up to Bullying, so that when the behaviors occur, we know just what to do.*

2. Show girls the pre-printed flipchart paper with *The Four Rules for STANding up to Bullying.*

3. Ask for a volunteer to read each of the rules aloud:

   ○ **S**how strength

   ○ **T**ell an adult

   ○ **A**ssert yourself

   ○ **N**ow!

4. *In learning about stopping rumors and using* Bully Bans, *you have already been practicing* Showing strength *and* Asserting yourselves. *Today, we will talk about how to use all four rules and put them together to* STANd up to Bullying *behavior effectively.*

5. It may be helpful to point out that the rules do not have to be followed in order. Rather they are designed to all work together to *STANd up to Bullying.*

6. Use the following to guide the learning:

   a. **S**how strength

      ▪ *Whenever you STANd up to Bullying, it is important to show strength.*

      ▪ *When we talk about showing strength, we don't mean flexing muscles or challenging a bully to arm wrestle. Rather, you can show your inner strength by using things like eye contact and a strong tone of voice.*

      ▪ *Recall when we learned about stopping rumors and using* Bully Bans, *we practiced looking each other in the eyes. Making eye contact is one of the best ways that you can show your inner strength to someone else.*

      ▪ *What kind of tone of voice do you want to use when STANding up to a bully?*

         □ Encourage girls to talk about effective volume, tone, and the distance they want to stand from the other person. It may help to role model several statements.

         □ Allow for volunteers to practice using their voices to show strength. Suggest a *Bully Ban,* such as "*Friends don't do that to friends,*" for girls to practice.

b. **T**ell an adult

- *Another rule for STANding up to Bullying is to tell an adult. Some bullies kick, punch, hit, and do other things that easily attract adult attention. The kinds of bullying behaviors that we've been talking about, however, are usually disguised as friendship and done so quietly that most adults don't even know what is going on. That is part of what makes girl bullying so hurtful and troublesome.*

- *When someone is repeatedly gossiping about you, leaving you out, teasing you, or bullying you in any way, it is important that you explain to a trustworthy adult what is happening.*

- *Some girls worry that they will be called a tattletale if they tell an adult what is going on. Guess what? That is exactly what the bully wants you to think! The bully is hoping to make you feel all alone and powerless. When you tell an adult about what is happening and get their support, you take your voice back. Telling an adult is one of the most important and powerful things you can do.*

- *Keep in mind that an adult's role is not always to rush in and solve the problem for kids. Sometimes, a grown up's best help comes from supporting kids and giving them the strength to STANd up for themselves.*

- *Can anyone share a time when an adult has helped you in a bullying situation?*

c. **A**ssert yourself

- *Does anyone know what the words "Assert yourself" mean?*
    - Ask for volunteers and affirm any definitions that are close to the true meaning.
    - Young children will likely be unfamiliar with the term, however, so it is helpful to clarify the definition.

- *When kids assert themselves, they use words to express their feelings in a direct and respectful way. The* Bully Bans *that we came up with last session are great examples of how to assert yourself, using simple, to-the-point statements.*

- *Assertiveness involves showing strength and includes behaviors that we just talked about like making good eye contact and speaking in an even tone of voice.*

- *Bullying is about aggressiveness—a kind of behavior that some people use to hurt others. When girls use bullying behaviors like the ones we listed last week—leaving people out, spreading rumors, etc.—they are being aggressive in indirect, disguised ways.*

- *When you assert yourself, you show the bully that you are not afraid of her and will not hide your feelings behind indirect bullying behaviors. You make it clear that you have a strong voice and know how to express yourself directly and powerfully.*

  d. **Now!**

  - *One of the biggest mistakes people make when they are up against a bully is to ignore repeated bullying and hope that the problem will go away.*

  - *Bullying usually becomes more serious when the bully realizes that her victim is not going to STANd up for herself.*

  - *STANding up to the bully sooner rather than later is the best way to keep a strong and powerful voice.*

Putting it all together: Hand STANds

1. Tell the girls that now that they have learned all four rules, they are going to create their own *Hand STANds*.

2. *Hand STANds* are tip sheets that graphically remind girls of the four rules while also providing each girl with the opportunity to generate a unique anti-bullying slogan. Most importantly, after a session in which the girls did a lot of listening, *Hand STANds* give the girls the chance to actively design, create, and express themselves visually.

3. For this activity, each girl will need a piece of unlined paper, a pencil for tracing their hand, crayons and/or markers for drawing, and a hard surface on which to write.

4. A sample *Hand STANd*, drawn by a seven-year-old girl, is provided on page 78.

5. Instructions:

   ° *First, trace your hand on the paper. If you need help, ask an adult or a partner to trace your hand for you.*

   ° *Next, in the palm of the handprint, write the words "STANd up to Bullying."*

- *On each of the four fingers (excluding the thumb), write down one of* The Four Rules for STANding up to Bullying.

- *In the thumb area, create your own original anti-bullying slogan.* It may help to provide examples, such as:

  - "Bullies never win."

  - "I like myself!"

- *Use the rest of the page to write examples of each rule. For example:*

  - *For* Show strength, *you might draw an eye or write "make good eye contact."*

  - *For* Tell an adult, *list a few trustworthy adults you know you can talk to.*

  - *For* Assert yourself, *give examples of* Bully Bans *you are likely to use.*

  - *For* Now!, *you could draw a clock.*

- *Be creative and have fun with this activity! When you are finished, you will have the chance to share your* Hand STANd *with the group.*

6. Allow 10–15 minutes for the girls to design their *Hand STANds*, then reconvene the group for sharing time.

7. Invite each girl to present her *Hand STANd* to the group, reading her slogan aloud and sharing her examples and designs.

8. Encourage the girls to support and affirm one another in this sharing process by clapping after each presentation.

9. Tell the girls that they will be taking their *Hand STANds* home, to share their learning with their family and to remind themselves each day about how to *STANd up to Bullying*.

Storytime: My Secret Bully

1. If time remains, the children's book *My Secret Bully* by Trudy Ludwig (2004) provides a great example of the use of the four rules for STANding up to a friend who has become a bully. Convey the following:

   - My Secret Bully *is a story about bullying, disguised as friendship.*

   - *It tells the tale of how Monica feels when her "friend" Katie begins to use many of the behaviors we have talked about so far in group—Shredders, gossip, and leaving Monica out.*

- *My Secret Bully* *also shows how Monica gets the support of a helpful adult and stands up for herself in a powerful way.*

- *As I read, listen to see if you have ever felt like Monica.*

2. Invite the girls to gather around you, sitting together on the floor or in chairs, as you read the book aloud. Ludwig's book includes suggested discussion questions at the end of the story. These questions may be used, in addition to the following:

    - *What kinds of bullying behaviors did Katie use?*

    - *How did these behaviors make Monica feel?*

    - *Who did Monica turn to for help? How can trustworthy adults make girls feel supported in times of bullying?*

    - *What kind of* Bully Ban *did Monica use?*

    - *How did Monica's use of a* Bully Ban *work out?*

    - *In this story, what did Monica learn about* Real Friendship Values*?*

    - *What did Monica do to choose healthier friendships?*

    - *How did Monica feel at the end of the story?*

    - *Can you relate to Monica's experiences? How?*

Session conclusion

- Affirm the girls for their attentive listening and creative participation:

    - *Today, we talked about how we can be successful in handling bullies, using* The Four Rules for STANding up to Bullying. *The* Hand STANds *we made can serve as ongoing reminders of how strong we can be.*

    - *Next week, we are going to talk even more about strength, as we do some fun activities to explore what makes each of us unique, strong, and special. When we are confident in our selves and in our abilities, we STANd up to bullies.*

Friendship Journal

1. Hand out the *Friendship Journal* (page 79).

2. Topic: *This week, think about the four rules for* STANding up to Bullying *and how they can be used in real life. Write or draw about a situation in which the four rules could be used. The situation can be real, imagined, or one you have read about or seen on TV.*

3. Remind girls that the purpose of this *Friendship Journal* assignment is to practice using the four rules in everyday life.

Customizing the curriculum

- In the opening activity, older participants may benefit from classifying the responses as passive (P), aggressive (AG), and/or passive aggressive (PA) behaviors. To make the activity more challenging, the facilitator can challenge the girls to list at least five "wrong way" responses for each category.

- Some girls will pick up quickly on concepts such as using body language to show strength and asserting themselves with simple, to-the-point *Bully Bans*, while others may need more time to process and practice each element of the STANd rules. Be attentive to participant ability levels and allow more or less time for practice, as necessary.

- As with the previous session, this one may be divided into two separate sessions if additional time is needed. A first session can feature expanded practice of the four STANd rules, while the follow-up can provide more time for the girls to create and present their *Hand STANds*.

✓

Handout: Hand STANd

Copyright © Signe Whitson 2012

Friendship Journal

This week, think about *The Four Rules for STANding up to Bullying* and how they can be used in real life. Write or draw about a situation in which the four rules could be used. The situation can be real, imagined, or one you have read about or seen on TV.

Letter to Parents

Dear Parents,

Today, in the *Real Friendship* group, your daughter learned four rules for *STANding up to Bullying* behavior. Ask her to show you the *Hand STANd* that she created, featuring the four rules, along with her original anti-bullying slogan. Your daughter's *Hand STANd* is a great keepsake and creative reminder of the importance of standing up to bullies.

At home, talk with your daughter about the four rules. Ask her to explain each one to you. "Teaching" you about handling bullying is one of the best ways for your daughter to strengthen her new skills. Continue to use role play to help her practice putting the four rules together. As you read, watch TV, and talk about everyday friendship experiences, point out situations in which *STANding up to Bullying* can work in real life.

It is not uncommon for girls to worry that if they STANd up for themselves that bullying might worsen. Encourage your daughter to discuss her thoughts and fears about asserting herself. Teach her that anger and friendship are not mutually exclusive; assertiveness skills can help girls express anger about a particular situation while still maintaining a friendship. Better yet, most girls find that they are more respected and less bullied when others know that they will not hesitate to STANd up for themselves.

Reading stories about other girls' experiences handling and overcoming bullying is a great way to reinforce new skills and remind your daughter that she is not alone in facing bullying. A list of recommended children's books on the subject of coping with bullying is provided below.

Recommended reading

Al Abdullah, Her Majesty Queen Rania (2010) *The Sandwich Swap*. New York: Disney Hyperion Books.

Bateman, T. (2004) *The Bully Blockers Club*. Chicago: Albert Whitman and Company.

Cuyler, M. (2007) *Kindness is Cooler, Mrs. Ruler*. New York: Simon and Schuster Children's Publishing.

Cuyler, M. (2009) *Bullies Never Win*. New York: Simon and Schuster Children's Publishing.

Kroll, S. (2006) *Jungle Bullies*. New York: Marshall Cavendish.

Ludwig, T. (2004) *My Secret Bully*. Berkeley: Tricycle Press.

Otoshi, K. (2008) *One*. San Raphael, CA: KO Kids Books.

Seskind, S. and Shamblin, A. (2002) *Don't Laugh at Me*. Berkeley, CA: Tricycle Press.

Session 6

Who Am I?
Exploring Personal Strengths

Session objectives

- To identify and explore individual strengths.
- To learn how knowing personal strengths can help a person withstand bullying.
- To practice building the self-esteem of fellow group members.

Materials needed

- flipchart paper and markers
- unlined paper for each participant
- pencils, crayons, and markers or any other art supplies for each participant
- hard surface for girls to complete drawing task
- masking tape for hanging completed *Self-Portraits*
- (optional) MP3 player with speakers, radio, or other way to play music during the Art Show.

Before beginning

- Prepare copies of the *Friendship Journal* (page 86) for each participant.
- Prepare copies of the *Letter to Parents* handout (page 87) for each participant to take home.

Welcome back

1. Welcome girls to the sixth group session. Let the girls know that the *Real Friendship* group has just reached the halfway mark. Affirm all of the participants' hard work and active learning during the first five group sessions.

2. Review last week's session on four rules for *STANding up to Bullying*. Ask for volunteers to name and give a quick explanation or example of each rule:

    ° *Show strength.* Use direct eye contact, an even tone of voice, etc.

    ° *Tell an adult.* Reach out to trustworthy adults that can provide help and support.

    ° *Assert yourself.* Use *Bully Bans.*

    ° *Now!* Don't wait before STANding up for yourself.

3. Preview this week's agenda:

    ° *So far in our sessions, we have focused on two very important things:*

        i. *How to recognize behaviors typical of girl bullying.*

        ii. *How to respond to bullying behaviors effectively.*

    ° *The third important part of developing Real Friendships is realizing all of the things that make you feel proud of who you are as a person.*

    ° *When you feel proud of yourself, you can withstand the hurtful behaviors of others.*

    ° *Today, we are going to focus on activities that help us discover the things that make us strong, proud, and bully-proof!*

Opening activity: I Feel Proud

1. Invite the girls to sit together in a circle. Let them know that this first activity will give each girl a chance to think about—and share—something they are proud of.

2. Each girl should begin a statement with the words, "*I feel proud when…*" and complete the sentence with an original thought.

3. Encourage girls to focus on statements that reflect pride in a specific skill, ability, or type of behavior, rather than on a physical trait.

4. The facilitator should begin the activity to role model an effective *"I feel proud when…"* statement.

5. Allow the activity to continue until each girl has had a chance to take a turn.

6. As a follow-up, ask the girls:

    ○ *How does it feel to talk about things that make you feel proud of yourself?*

    ○ *Did you learn anything new about another girl in the group during this activity?*

Self-Portraits

1. In this activity, each girl will be given the chance to draw a self-portrait. When the portraits are completed, the girls will hang them around the room and engage in an "Art Show" set to music. The purpose of this activity is to allow the girls to express their strengths creatively and to have the experience of receiving positive feedback from their peers. Convey the instructions as follows:

    ○ *On your paper, create a self-portrait. A self-portrait is a picture that you draw of yourself. It should represent not just how you look physically, but things about you that make you feel proud.*

    ○ *For example, you might draw yourself with a book if you enjoy reading, or with a soccer ball if you love to play soccer.*

    ○ *Your portrait can also include words or phrases, such as "sister," "smart," or "loves music" to share other proud parts of yourself.*

    ○ *After your portrait is finished, we will hang them around the room and have an "Art Show" for everyone to share their work.*

2. Supply the girls with crayons, markers, and any other available art supplies to complete their self-portrait. Allow up to 15 minutes for the girls to create their portraits.

3. As each girl finishes, hang their portrait along a wall in the group room. Next to each self-portrait, hang a blank piece of paper. This paper will be used for group members to write compliments to one another about the self-portraits.

4. Have a music player available to play music during the Art Show (see instructions on the following page).

5. Art Show instructions:

    ◦   *To begin the Art Show, stand in front of a portrait that is not your own. Each of you should choose a different portrait to stand in front of first. You will each have a chance to visit every portrait during the Art Show.*

    ◦   *I will be playing music while you browse at the art. While the music is playing, your job is to write a compliment to the artist about their self-portrait. Use the blank paper next to each portrait to write your positive comments.*

    ◦   *Every time the music stops, finish up the compliment you are writing and move on to the next portrait in the Art Show.*

    ◦   *Take your time to give each girl a genuine compliment on her work. When we feel proud of ourselves and supported by our friends, we are all better able to stand up to bullying.*

6. When each girl has visited each portrait, allow the girls to return to their own portraits and read the compliments that have been written.

7. Encourage discussion about the activity:

    ◦   *How did it feel to read what others wrote on your portrait?*

    ◦   *Did you know that other people appreciated these things about you?*

    ◦   *How did it feel to give compliments to others?*

    ◦   *Does it ever make you feel good to make someone else feel good? Why?*

8. Wrap up the activity by reminding girls that when they know their own strengths and feel proud of themselves, it is hard for a bully to make them feel bad about themselves.

9. If space allows, keep the portraits hung in the group room over the course of the next several sessions. Encourage the girls to continue to browse through the portraits in weeks to come, to see what has been written about other girls and to remind themselves of the compliments they have received from others.

10. If space does not allow, the girls should be invited to take home their portrait and hang it at home, as a reminder of the things that help them feel strong and proud about themselves.

Session conclusion

- *So far in the group, we have learned about* recognizing *bully behavior,* responding *to it effectively, and* realizing *our own strengths. All of these things put together help us to develop* Real Friendships.

- *In the next few sessions, we are going to talk more about* Real Friendships, *including how to choose healthy friendships and how to be an ally to other girls who are facing bullying.*

Friendship Journal

1. Hand out the *Friendship Journal* (page 86).

2. Topic: *This week, continue thinking about the things that make you feel strong and proud. In your Journal, write your first name with the letters going vertically down the page. For each letter, write a word or phrase that describes something you are proud of.*

3. *Example:*
   - **E**xcellent artist
   - **L**ikes roller skating
   - **I** love my family
   - **S**inging
   - **E**njoys nature.

Customizing the curriculum

- The activities in this session are universal across wide age spans—even parents may enjoy sharing their personal strengths with their daughters as part of at-home reinforcement of group skills. While no major modifications are suggested, it can be helpful to customize the available art supplies, accompanying music, and time for presenting self-portraits, based on participant needs.

✓

Friendship Journal

This week, continue thinking about the things that make you feel strong and proud. In your Journal, write your first name with the letters going vertically down the page. For each letter, write a word or phrase that describes something you are proud of.

Letter to Parents

Dear Parents,

Your daughter helped put on an Art Show! You are cordially invited to join in the celebration of her personal strengths by checking out the self-portrait she created in the *Real Friendship* group.

Today, the girls learned that being proud of their personal strengths can help them withstand the hurtful behavior of others. In our opening activity, each girl took turns identifying at least one thing that makes her feel proud of herself. Ask your daughter to tell you about the "*I feel proud when…*" statement she shared with the group.

The girls created self-portraits to explore additional things that make them feel strong and proud. The portraits were hung in an Art Show and each girl had the chance to give and receive positive feedback. When girls feel the support of friends and family, they are better able to stand up to bullying.

For her *Friendship Journal* this week, your daughter will continue to think about the things that make her feel strong and proud. Her assignment is to write a word or phrase that describes something she is proud of, to correspond with each letter of her first name.

Another memorable, at-home self-esteem builder is to ask your daughter to pick ten positive words to describe herself. She should write the words down as a list. Next, check out www.wordle.net. When your daughter enters the ten positive words, the website automatically generates a word cloud, or a "Wordle." The whole family can take turns generating these creative representations of their personal strengths, featured in various colors and fonts. Wordles can even be printed and shared with friends.

Sharing your own personal strengths is a great way to become actively involved with your daughter in this week's topic. Talk about the things that make you feel strong and proud. Make this a regular part of your family's dinner or bedtime rituals. When family members share a simple "*I feel proud when…*" statement each day, unique strengths are reinforced, confidence builds from within, and your child grows in her ability to withstand hurtful behaviors in the outside world.

I Feel Connected
Finding Common Ground and Celebrating Differences

Session objectives

- To explore similarities and differences among group members.

- To learn about how connection offers support and protection from bullying.

Materials needed

- flipchart paper and markers

- wooden craft sticks

- colored construction (sugar) paper, cut into 2-inch strips

- pens or pencils for each participant

- glue stick or stapler

- (optional) copy of the book *The Sandwich Swap*, by Her Majesty Queen Rania Al Abdullah of Jordan (2010).

Before beginning

- Prepare three paper strips for each participant.

- Prepare copies of the *Friendship Journal* (page 95) for each participant.

- Prepare copies of the *Letter to Parents* handout (page 96) for each participant to take home.

Welcome back

1. Welcome girls to the seventh group session.

2. Review last week's session on exploring personal strengths and feeling proud of yourself.

    ◦ Ask for volunteers to share their *Friendship Journals*, in which the girls wrote something they were proud of, for each letter of their first name.

3. Preview this week's agenda:

    ◦ *This week, we are going to focus on the ways that we are all connected, through both our similarities and our differences.*

    ◦ *When we are connected, we are protected* (emphasize the rhyming words) *from bullying.*

Opening activity: Linking Arms

In this first activity, girls will practice asking questions of one another to find things they have in common. When they discover a similarity, they will link arms. The activity continues until the entire group is linked together, arm-in-arm.

The purpose of the activity is threefold:

•   to teach girls how to look for common ground

•   to show girls that similarities often lie below the surface (e.g. not just physical characteristics)

•   to understand that connectedness can protect girls from the negative effects of bullying.

1. Arrange the girls in a standing up circle and explain the activity rules as follows:

    ◦ *When it is your turn, ask questions of the girl on your right to discover something that the two of you have in common.*

    ◦ *The only rule is that the questions cannot be about a similarity that you already know of (e.g. Are you in my* Real Friendship *group?) or about a similarity you can see (e.g. Do we both have blonde hair?). Rather, the questions should aim to discover a shared like, dislike, hobby, or interest (e.g. Do you like to stay up late at night? Do you like chocolate ice cream?).*

    ◦   *When you discover a similarity, link arms with the girl. Then, it is her turn to ask questions and discover common ground with the next girl in the circle.*

    ◦   *The activity will continue until we are all linked by our similarities.*

2. The facilitator should initiate the first round of questioning, to role model the activity for the girls.

3. Once the activity has been completed and all of the girls are linked together, the facilitator should affirm everyone's participation. Ask the girls to look around the connected circle and think for a moment about how the process of looking for similarities brought the entire group together.

4. Use the following questions to guide a follow-up discussion:

    ◦   *Was it hard or easy to discover common ground with another girl?*

    ◦   *How did it feel to discover new similarities with someone?*

    ◦   *Were you surprised at some of the things you have in common with other girls?*

    ◦   *Was there ever a time in your life when you met someone and thought you were complete opposites, but then realized that you actually had some things in common?*

    ◦   *How can knowing how to find similarities with a girl help you to establish a friendship and protect both girls from bullying?*

5. As a wrap-up to this activity, the facilitator should emphasize that bullying behavior often aims to make girls feel like they are all alone. Knowing how to connect with others—by finding similarities and common ground—is a great way to protect yourself from the hurtful effects of bullying.

6. It might be helpful to flipchart the phrase: *"Connection Gives Protection."*

Differences: Chain Links

This second activity highlights the flipside of friendship: connecting through an appreciation of differences.

1. Convey the following:

    ◦   *When we first meet a new person, similarities might not be easy to find.*

    ◦   *In fact, sometimes we might assume that we have nothing at all in common with a person and, therefore, can't become friends.*

    ◦   *Even when common ground isn't so easy to find, sometimes the very best—and most interesting—friendships are those based on the things that make us different from our friends.*

     ○ *In this next activity, we are going to link together once more—this time by exploring our differences.*

2. Arrange the girls in small groups of 3–4, using the *Craft Stick Method* (see page 21).

3. Give each girl three strips of colored paper and a pencil.

4. Challenge the girls to talk and ask questions of the members of their small group in order to identify at least three ways that each girl is different from every other girl in the group. This time, the differences can include physical characteristics (e.g. *I have red hair*) but the focus should remain on hobbies, interests, talents, etc.

5. Each time a girl discovers something that makes her unique within her group, she should write it on one of the strips of paper.

6. When each girl has finished writing on all three of her strips, the group members should use a stapler or glue stick to create circular links from their paper strips and to connect all of their links into a single chain.

7. When the small groups have completed their task, the facilitator should bring all of the girls back together and encourage them to connect all of their small group links into a single large group chain.

     ○ *In our first group activity we saw how easy it was to find common ground and connect through our similarities. Now, we can see how we are also linked by our differences.*

     ○ *When we remember all of the ways through which we are connected—both in our similarities and our differences—we understand how we can feel protected from the hurtful effects of bullying.*

8. If the group space permits, hang or drape the *Differences Chain* in an easily visible location in the room and encourage girls to look at it during upcoming sessions, to remind themselves of how we are united, even in our differences.

Storytime: The Sandwich Swap

- If time remains, a great children's story for celebrating both similarities and differences in girl friendships is *The Sandwich Swap*, by Her Majesty Queen Rania Al Abdullah of Jordan (2010).

- *The Sandwich Shop* is the heartwarming and easily relatable tale of Salma and Lily, two best friends united by common interests, but then abruptly pulled apart by differences in their school lunches. In the end, the girls learn a powerful lesson about friendship—and show an entire community how to come together.

- Arrange the girls in a sitting circle as you read *The Sandwich Shop* aloud. The following discussion questions may be helpful:

  ○ *What were some of the things Salma and Lily shared in common?*

  ○ *What was the one difference that tore the friends apart?*

  ○ *Why did a difference in lunches cause a problem in their friendship?*

  ○ *What could the girls have done to avoid hurting each other over sandwich preferences?*

  ○ *How did Salma and Lily's fight effect the other kids in their school?*

  ○ *How did Salma and Lily make up?*

  ○ *In the end, were Salma and Lily's preferences in sandwiches really that different?*

  ○ *What did Salma and Lily teach their classmates by the end of the story?*

Session conclusion

- *This week, we discovered that we are all connected in important ways, both through the things we have in common with one other and the qualities that make us unique.*

- *We learned that* Connection Gives Protection *and that knowing how to link with supportive friends can help us withstand bullying behavior.*

- *Next week, we will talk about connecting with and supporting other girls when we know that they are being bullied.*

Friendship Journal

1. Hand out the *Friendship Journal* (page 95).

2. Topic: *Talk with a friend who is not in the* Real Friendship *group. Ask her questions to find several things that you and she share in common. Also, try to come up with 2–3 ways that you are different from one another. Write or draw about the special connection you share with this friend.*

3. The purpose of this activity is to encourage the girls to continue to think about similarities and differences in friendship and how both can create powerful and protective connections.

Customizing the curriculum

*   Younger participants may have difficulty thinking of questions to ask one another to discover similarities and differences. If that is the case, the facilitator can suggest helpful questions and/or allow girls to use questions based on visible physical characteristics.

*   For older girls, make it more of a challenge to discover similarities and differences. Rule out visible physical characteristics from the list of questions and consider increasing the number of chain links that the girls create during the *Differences: Chain Links* activity (see page 91).

*   To add an extra degree of difficulty, challenge older girls to identify a characteristic that makes them unique from anyone in the room, not just their small group. Challenge girls to talk about their heritage, hobbies, or other low-risk personal information that makes them feel proud of their uniqueness. This challenge can be tied in to the lesson on personal strengths from the previous session.

Friendship Journal

Talk with a friend who is not in the *Real Friendship* group. Ask her questions to find several things that you and she share in common. Also, try to come up with 2–3 ways that you are different from one another. Write or draw about the special connection you share with this friend.

Letter to Parents

Dear Parents,

Connection Gives Protection. This is the simple rhyme your daughter discussed today in the *Real Friendship* group, as girls participated in activities to learn about how they are linked through both their similarities and their differences.

In the first activity the girls practiced looking for common ground with one another and learned that, since important similarities often lie below the surface, it is helpful to use questions to get to know others. Ask your daughter to tell you about the things she found out she has in common with other group members. Encourage her to talk about how this type of connection can bolster friendship.

In the second activity of the day the girls learned that even when common ground isn't so easy to find, sometimes the very best—and most interesting—friendships are those based on the things that make the girls different from their friends. Each girl identified three ways that she is unique from other group members. Then, the girls built a *Differences Chain* to emphasize how group members are linked by their differences, as well as by the things that make them alike.

In the end, the message was clear: bullying aims to make girls feel as though they are all alone, but knowing how to connect with others—by finding similarities and celebrating differences—is a great way to protect girls from bullying.

At home, talk with your daughter about ways to connect with other kids. Practice conversation starters and role play ways to successfully accept and manage differences. A great children's book for encouraging discussion about similarities and differences in friendship is *The Sandwich Swap* by Her Majesty Queen Rania Al Abdullah (2010).

Don't Just Stand There!
Three Occasions for Becoming an Ally

Session objectives

- To learn about the power of peer support in helping girls stay strong in the face of bullying.

- To learn how and when to become an ally to someone who is being bullied.

Materials needed

- six wooden craft sticks for each participant

- pen or marker for each participant

- flipchart paper and markers

- art supplies for creating *Becoming an Ally* poster campaigns.

Before beginning

- Pre-print flipchart paper with the title "*Becoming an Ally.*"

- Prepare copies of the *Becoming an Ally* handout (page 104).

- Prepare copies of the *Friendship Journal* (page 106) for each participant.

- Prepare copies of the *Letter to Parents* handout (page 107) for each participant to take home.

Welcome back

1. Welcome girls to the eighth group session.

2. Review last week's session on connectedness:

    ○ *Who can recall the rhyme we used to talk about the power of connection in* Real Friendships*?* (Connection Gives Protection.)

    ○ *We discovered that as a group of girls, we are connected and protected both by the things that we have in common and by the things that make us entirely unique.*

    ○ *What kinds of connections were you able to make with others this week by looking for similarities? Differences?*

3. Preview this week's agenda:

    ○ *So far in our sessions we have talked about the kinds of behaviors that bullies use and we have learned about what to do if you are being bullied. There is one more important person we need to talk about: the person(s) who witnesses the bullying.*

    ○ *Today we are going to pull together information from several of our previous sessions—lessons on STANding up to bullies and the protection of connection—to talk about what to do if you know that someone is being bullied.*

Opening activity: Craft Sticks

In this memorable icebreaker activity, girls will use a simple physics demonstration to learn firsthand about the power of peer support in helping girls stay strong in the face of bullying.

1. Give each girl six craft sticks (ice lolly sticks).

2. Tell the girls to write their name on the first stick.

3. Once everyone has done this, challenge each girl to break their stick in half. This should be easy to do, with ordinary craft sticks.

4. Observe aloud for the girls:

    ○ *On its own, the stick is easy to break.*

    ○ *Now, let's see what happens when that stick gets some help from its friends.*

5. Tell the girls to write their name again on one of the five unbroken craft sticks. On a second stick, write the phrase *"STANding up to Bullies."* Then, on each of the three remaining sticks, challenge the girls to write the name of someone in their life who they know they can always count on for support, friendship, and love. They can write the names of family members, teachers, friends, and even pets!

6. Once the girls have written on all five craft sticks, assign them to stack the sticks, placing the stick with their name on it on top of the stack. Then challenge the girls to try to break the craft sticks while they are stacked together.

7. The task should be impossible—and also quite surprising—for the girls. Use this "dramatic" experiment to convey the following points about supportive relationships:

   ○ *On its own, the craft stick was easy to break.*

   ○ *When girls have skills for STANding up to bullies and the support of others, they become unbreakable!*

   ○ *The skills you are learning in this* Real Friendship *group will keep you strong anytime you face bullying.*

   ○ *Keep these craft sticks as a reminder of how strong you truly are.*

Becoming an Ally

In this activity, girls will learn how to become supportive allies for one another anytime they witness or have knowledge of bullying behavior.

1. Write the words, *"Becoming an Ally"* on a piece of flipchart paper. Explain the concept in your own words:

   ○ *In most bullying situations, there are at least three people. Who can name one of them?*

   ▪ Most often, kids will readily list the bully and the person being bullied.

   ▪ If girls do not come up with it on their own, encourage them to also cite the bystander/witness/person who has knowledge of the bullying.

   ○ *If the bystander does not do anything to actually hurt the bullied person, is she guilty of doing anything wrong?*

2. There may be mixed responses to this question. Of course, there is some gray area as to "degree of guilt." For the purposes of this group, it is helpful to present these decisive teaching points about *Becoming an Ally*.

    ○   *This group is all about developing* Real Friendships *in which girls help and support one another. In one of our first sessions, we listed* Behaviors that Are Hurtful to Friendship *(page 63) and committed not to use those types of behaviors. Now, to become true allies, we need to agree not to stand by if we ever see or have knowledge of someone else using them.*

    ○   *It is never okay to do nothing when you know that bullying is happening. If you see bullying happen or have knowledge about it, it is up to you to do what is right and to be an ally to a girl who needs your support.*

    This is a critical point. Pause to let the message sink in.

3. It may be helpful to flipchart a phrase such as "*It is never okay to do nothing about bullying.*"

    ○   *What are some of the reasons that girls might stand by and do nothing, even when they know that bullying is taking place?* Allow for a few responses, such as:

        ▪   Fear of the bully: if I stand up for someone, the bully might turn on me.

        ▪   The bully is my friend: I don't like what she is doing, but she is still my friend.

        ▪   The person being bullied is not my friend.

        ▪   I barely know the person being bullied.

        ▪   I don't know how to stop the bully.

4. Affirm all of the responses and assure the girls that they are not alone in their reasoning:

    ○   *There are many real and powerful reasons why people stand by and do not act to stop bullying.*

    ○   *In this group, however, you are learning how to be stronger, bolder, and more empathic than someone who would simply stand by and watch someone else be mistreated.*

    ○   *You have a strong voice and you know how to use it.*

    ○   *Instead of being a bystander, you can become an ally.*

    ○   *When you act like an ally, you actively support other girls and keep them strong in the face of bullying.*

- Use the craft stick stack as a visual reinforcement of your words.

  ○ *Let's talk about three times when you can* Become an Ally.

5. On flipchart paper, write the words "*Before,*" "*During,*" and "*After.*"

6. Tell the girls that they can *Become an Ally* at any point in a bullying situation—before the bullying occurs, during an actual episode of bullying, and even after the fact.

7. Lead a brainstorming activity in which the girls name specific behaviors they can use at any of the three points. A *Becoming an Ally* handout is provided on page 104. Use the handout to guide the brainstorming session as necessary. Then, after the brainstorming activity, give each girl a copy of the handout to take home.

8. Affirm the girls' participation in brainstorming the Before/During/After of *Becoming an Ally*. If it has not been mentioned previously in this activity, remind them of this phrase: *Connection Gives Protection.*

Ally Posters

In this final activity of the session, the girls will have an opportunity to express their new knowledge about allies in a creative way.

1. Explain the activity as follows:

   ○ *We have come a long way in this group. Now is your chance to start passing on your new knowledge to others.*

   ○ *Create an original poster that represents the importance of* Becoming an Ally *in a bullying situation.*

   ○ *This poster should help other girls get an idea of how important it is to stop bullying whenever they see it and to show that* Real Friendship *means standing up for girls who are bullied.*

2. Give each girl a piece of flipchart paper or poster board, along with markers and any other available art supplies. Use the remaining group time to allow the girls to work on a poster. Encourage the use of slogans and/or any of the phrases, rules, etc. that have been discussed in the *Real Friendship* group.

3. Save enough time at the end of the session for each girl to present her poster to the group. If any of the girls do not have time to finish their poster, allow them to take the poster home and finish it over the course of the next week.

4. Hang any finished posters around the group room. If possible in your setting, arrange for the posters to be hung in a hallway or common area where larger audiences can view the *Becoming an Ally* poster campaign.

Session conclusion

- *This week, we learned that when girls have skills for STANding up to bullies and the support of others, they become unbreakable!*

- *We learned that it is never okay to do nothing about bullying and talked about ways to become an ally before, during, and after bullying situations. Our* Becoming an Ally *posters are a great visual reminder of the importance of supporting friends at all times.*

- *Next week, we will talk about two very important values when it comes to* Real Friendship.

Friendship Journal

1. Hand out the *Friendship Journal* (page 106).

2. Topic: *Have you ever acted like an ally for a friend who was facing bullying? Draw or write about a time when you shared your strength with a person in need. If you haven't had this experience yet, share some of the ways that you will act like an ally in the future, when needed.*

3. The purpose of this assignment is to encourage the girls to apply the skills discussed in the group to real world situations.

Customizing the curriculum

- Unlike many of the other elements in this curriculum in which activities need to be modified to accommodate younger participants, in the case of *Becoming an Ally*, it is usually older girls who have more difficulty. As girls age, they feel increasingly intense pressure to conform to social hierarchies and not attract the attention of bullies who could turn their wrath on them. When talking about the reasons that girls might stand by and do nothing to counter bullying, be sensitive to older girls' very real fears about *Becoming an Ally*, while still reinforcing the importance of doing so.

- Giving girls concrete strategies for *Becoming an Ally* before, during, and after bullying situations can help make the skill of standing up for others seem more achievable. Likewise, framing ally behavior in terms of a bold move based on *Friendship Values* is a great way to encourage girls to be willing to adopt this seemingly risky behavior.

✓

Handout: Becoming an Ally

Facilitator notes

This list can be used to supplement participant brainstorming during the Becoming an Ally *discussion.*

Before

When you become aware that bullying will take place (e.g. you overhear a conversation or are the recipient of gossip) you can:

- refuse to spread the gossip

- tell the person to stop spreading rumors and gossip

- tell an adult about what you overhear

- reach out to the girl who is being targeted. Offer to sit with her at lunch, play with her at recess, or help her feel connected to friends in another way

- remind the bully about important friendship values.

During

When you see or hear bullying taking place (e.g. someone is being excluded at a lunch table or being teased) you can:

- use a *Bully Ban* to stand up for the person being bullied

- tell an adult about what is going on

- reach out to the girl being bullied. Help her feel the protection of connection with friends by talking with her, including her in your group of friends, sitting with her, etc.

- act quickly. Don't wait for the bully to hurt or humiliate the girl before you stand up for her. Your strength and action will show others that it is never okay to do nothing about bullying.

After

When you find out that someone you know has been bullied, you can:

- listen to her as she talks about her feelings

- tell her that you are sorry about what happened to her

- encourage her to reach out to a trustworthy adult

- go with her to talk to an adult

- teach her *The Four Rules for STANding up to Bullying* and help her practice the rules

- make sure to include her in activities with your group of friends.

✓

Friendship Journal

Have you ever acted like an ally for a friend who was facing bullying? Draw or write about a time when you shared your strength with a person in need. If you haven't had this experience yet, share some of the ways that you will act like an ally in the future, when needed.

Letter to Parents

Dear Parents,

Your daughter has learned so much in the *Real Friendship* group. She understands how to recognize bullying behavior, even when it is disguised as friendship, and she knows how to STANd up for herself. She has practiced celebrating her own strengths and has also learned the importance of connecting with supportive friends and family members. Ask your daughter to tell you (or better yet, show you) what she learned in group today about how her family members and friends help her to become "unbreakable."

In today's *Real Friendship* group, the girls learned about one more important person in most bullying dynamics: the person who witnesses the bullying. Though the group members talked about the reasons why some girls act as bystanders and fail to STANd up for others, they also learned that *in Real Friendship, it is never okay to do nothing about bullying.* The girls learned specific strategies for *Becoming an Ally* to a person who is bullied before, during, and after the bullying takes place. Talk with your daughter about how she can *Become an Ally* at each of these three points.

To reinforce the concept of the power of allies, check out the multi-award winning children's book, *One* by author Kathryn Otoshi (2008). Use role play to help your daughter practice acting like an ally. When you see bullying behavior acted out on TV, in movies, or played out in real life, make a point of talking with your daughter about what could be done to reach out to the victim. Show your daughter through your own actions that when a person needs help, you will be the one to stand up and offer your assistance and friendship. The power of role modeling is second to none when it comes to teaching children how to reach out to others.

Standing in Your Shoes
Fostering Empathy and Cooperation in Girls

Session objectives

- To learn about how cooperation is more effective than competition in meeting participants' best interests.

- To define "Empathy" and learn how this *Friendship Value* can help girls resolve conflicts and build friendships.

Materials needed

- jump rope (skipping rope)

- masking tape

- watch or other timer

- small prizes or candy treats (sweets) for all participants

- colored construction (sugar) paper large enough for the girls to trace their shoes

- child-safe scissors

- pencils or pens

- wooden craft sticks.

Before beginning

- Pre-print the rules for the *Pull the Rope* activity, as follows:

  ◦ This game will be played in 30-second rounds.

- When I say "Go!" begin pulling on your end of the rope.

- Each time you pull your partner over the middle line, you will receive a treat.

- Prepare the *Empathy Role Plays* handout (pages 115 and 116).

- Prepare copies of the *Friendship Journal* (page 117) for each participant

- Prepare copies of the *Letter to Parents* handout (page 118) for each participant to take home.

Welcome back

1. Welcome girls to the ninth group session.

2. Review last week's session on *Becoming an Ally*.

   - *Last week we learned that it is never okay to do nothing about bullying.*

   - *Who can name two actions that an ally can take before an incident of bullying even occurs? During an incident? After an incident?*

   - *What would it mean to you to have a girl be your ally in a bullying situation?*

3. Preview this week's agenda:

   - *This week, we are going to focus on two of the* Friendship Values *that we identified in our first session. In the second half of the group, we will talk about empathy and the skill of being able to see the world through someone else's point of view.*

   - *For our first activity, it is more helpful to experience the value than to describe it...*

Opening activity: Pull the Rope

Call it instinct, call it human nature; it often seems as if kids are naturally wired to compete with one another. While competition plays a healthy role in some aspects of kids' lives, when it comes to friendship, cooperation is often a more constructive value. This activity is designed to show girls how cooperation can serve the best interests of all of the group members.

1. Select two volunteers to play each other in a rope-pulling game. Take care to pick two girls who seem evenly matched in size and strength.

2. Clear a space in the room and mark a middle line on the floor with a piece of masking tape.

3. Give each girl one end of a jump rope and position the girls an even distance from the taped middle line.

4. Show the girls a flipchart, pre-printed with these rules:

   ◦ This game will be played in 30-second rounds.

   ◦ When I say "Go!" begin pulling on your end of the rope.

   ◦ Each time you pull your partner over the middle line, you will receive a treat. (The facilitator can choose to give small candy treats or other small prize items.)

   If participants have questions about the activity, you may answer them. Otherwise the rules should remain as simple as possible at this point.

5. When both volunteers are ready, begin the first 30-second round.

6. Because kids are so accustomed to competing during games, the girls will almost always use the 30 seconds to pull against each other.

7. After the first round of play, ask questions to encourage the girls to think about how a *cooperative* approach to play could have better suited their interests:

   ◦ *What was the point of this game?*

     ▪ The girls will most likely indicate some version of a competitive goal.

     ▪ Refer to the pre-printed flipchart to demonstrate that the activity rules did not specify this as a competitive activity.

   ◦ *Is there a different way the game could have been played, so that each girl could have won more prizes?*

     ▪ Encourage the girls to think about using a cooperative approach, such as agreeing to step back and forth over the middle line as many times as possible during the 30 seconds.

     ▪ Allow a second round of play, in which the girls can compare the relative merits of a cooperative approach versus the competitive one.

8. If the girls do take a cooperative approach within the first round, the facilitator should affirm their cooperative instincts and simply emphasize how a cooperative strategy met both girls' best interests.

9. Provide small candy treats or prizes for all group members to share at the end of the second round.

10. Emphasize that in friendship, cooperation usually serves everyone's best interests much more effectively than competition.

Standing in Someone Else's Shoes

In the second activity of the day, the girls are going to take part in an activity to practice developing empathy.

1. Ask the girls if they are familiar with the word "Empathy." Allow volunteers to suggest definitions using words or an example. Encourage girls to understand "Empathy" as the ability to put themselves in another person's shoes and to understand how that person is feeling in a particular situation.

2. If "Empathy" or "Understands How I Feel" was listed among the *Friendship Values* defined during the second group session (see page 42), it can be helpful to revisit the flipcharted list at this point, for emphasis.

    ◦ Likewise, if "Cooperation" is on the original *Real Friendship Values* list, this can be a key time to emphasize how the lessons of this *Real Friendship* group often return to the group's shared values.

3. Tell the girls that in order to practice using empathy with one another, they are going to get to—literally—stand in someone else's shoes.

4. Give each girl a pencil and enough colored construction paper to trace both of her footprints. Allow girls several minutes to create and cut out their own footprints. Ask each girl to write her name on both footprints.

5. Once all of the footprints have been cut out, use the *Craft Stick Method* (see page 21) to arrange the girls into pairs. (If there is an odd number of girls, use *Role Play 2: Isabella, Carly and Ava* from page 116.)

6. Have the girls set their footprints on the ground, so that they are standing face to face with their partner.

7. Give each pair of girls one of the *Empathy Role Plays* (pages 115 and 116). One girl should receive Role A and the other should receive Role B. Explain Round 1 of the activity:

    ◦ *Read the role that has been given to you. The girl with Role A should go first, acting out her point of view. When she is done, the girl with Role B should answer, acting out her different point of view.*

- *Go back and forth for 2–3 rounds, each insisting on your own perspective.*

- *Stop what you are doing when the facilitator says "Freeze."*

8. After Round 1 is complete, ask the girls to step away from their footprints and "into the shoes" of their partner. Tell the girls:

   - *You have not only stepped into the shoes of your partner, but you are also going to switch roles with her.*

   - *For Round 2, try taking the opposite point of view from the one you just played. If you just played Role A, you will now play Role B. If you played Role B before, act out Role A now.*

   - *Do this for 2–3 rounds, then stop when the facilitator says "Freeze."*

9. After the second round, ask the girls to remain standing in their partner's shoes. Encourage discussion about how it felt to take on a new point of view during the activity:

   - *How did it feel to play the first role you were assigned?*

   - *How did it feel when you had to walk in someone else's shoes and take on the perspective you had just argued with?*

   - *How can "standing in someone else's shoes" help you build* Real Friendship *bonds?*

   - *Was there ever a time in your life when you were able to solve a conflict by empathizing—or agreeing to see something from someone else's point of view? Explain.*

10. Wrap up the discussion by emphasizing that when girls are willing to step out of their own shoes and see the world from another person's perspective, they take giant steps in resolving conflicts and building friendships.

Session conclusion

- *This week, we learned that, in developing* Real Friendships, *it is important to try to stand in someone else's shoes.*

- *The next time you find yourself in a conflict with a friend, challenge yourself to see the world from their point of view and try to understand their thoughts and feelings.*

- *When you practice the values of cooperation and empathy, you will usually find that all of your interests are better served and that your friendships improve.*

- *Next week, we will talk about the value of including others and talk about how painful it can feel to be excluded from a group.*

Friendship Journal

1. Hand out the *Friendship Journal* (page 117).

2. Topic: *Write or draw about an occasion where you and a friend both benefitted from cooperating on a task. What was the task? How did you both benefit? What might have happened if you had competed instead?*

3. The purpose of this assignment is to encourage girls to think about applying group lessons about the value of cooperation into their daily lives. A separate task to focus on empathy development is suggested in the *Letter to Parents* (page 118).

Customizing the curriculum

- The *Pull the Rope* game can be modified in many ways to suit the abilities of the group and the materials on hand. Substitute scoring goals, tic tac toe wins, or any other game in which participants can help each other win, in order to both benefit from a prize.

- The facilitator should determine the relevance of each *Empathy Role Play* prior to the activity. The role plays can be edited, omitted and/or replaced with scenarios most relevant to the girls' everyday experiences.

- Older girls may want to use scenarios from their real life during the *Standing in Someone Else's Shoes* activity. As long as no identifiable information is included, allowing girls to write their own scenarios can make the experience more meaningful.

Activity: Empathy Role Plays

Facilitator notes

For each pair of girls, hand out version A and B of one of the Empathy Role Plays below. Instruct each girl to act out their roles with one another. After 1–2 minutes, say "Freeze." Have the girls swap roles and reverse positions, so that they are literally standing in their partner's shoe prints. Allow an additional 1–2 minutes for the girls to act out the new version of their Empathy Role Play.

Role Plays 1–2 are based on typical real-life events for young girls. Role Play 3 is based on the children's story Goldilocks and the Three Bears. *Sometimes, young children are better able to understand concepts like empathy when drawing upon fairy-tale situations.*

Role Play 1: Kristin and Mikayla

Version A: Kristin

You and Mikayla are drawing together. You ask Mikayla to pass you a black marker, so that you can color in your picture of a penguin. Mikayla refuses to share the black marker. You feel angry that Mikayla won't share. You can't finish your picture of a penguin without a black marker.

Version B: Mikayla

You and Kristin are drawing together. Kristin asks you to pass her a black marker, so that she can color in her picture of a penguin. Your older sister loaned you the set of markers and gave you a stern warning not to let anyone else use them. You are worried about making your sister angry, but you don't want to tell Kristin that you are scared of your sister.

Role Play 2: Isabella, Carly and Ava

This role play is written for a small group of three girls. Two girls share Version A, while one girl takes Version B.

Version A: Isabella and Carly

You and your friend are walking together, talking about a funny episode of a television program you both watched the night before. You each laugh out loud about one of the funny scenes. When you pass your friend Ava in the school hallway, you both wave to her.

Version B: Ava

You are walking in the hallway at school. You watch Isabella and Carly look at you and then begin to laugh. As they pass you, they look your way, wave and continue laughing with each other. You know they are making fun of you and feel hurt.

Role Play 3: Goldilocks and Little Bear

Version A: Little Bear

You and your parents went out for a walk in the woods, to allow your porridge time to cool. When you came home, you discovered that your bowl of porridge had been completely eaten up. To make matters worse, your favorite chair was smashed into pieces. All you wanted to do was crawl back into bed, but when you got there, you found a strange girl lying in it. Out of frustration, you let out a loud growl. The little blonde girl ran right out of the house, without even apologizing!

Version B: Goldilocks

You and your parents went for a walk in the woods. You stopped to pick a wildflower. When you started walking again, your parents were nowhere to be found! Scared, you walked around looking for them until you came upon a house. You knocked on the door, but no one answered. Cold, tired, hungry, and hoping to find someone who could help you, you entered the house. Having not eaten breakfast yet, you couldn't resist taking a bite of the warm porridge on the table. Before you knew it, you had eaten it all. You sat down on a little chair to think about what to do. Suddenly, the chair broke into pieces. You walked upstairs to try to tell someone what had happened. The last thing you remember, you laid down to rest for just a moment, when suddenly an angry bear roared. You ran for your life, right past the bear, out of the house, and back through the woods. You had never been so scared in your life!

Friendship Journal

Write or draw about an occasion where you and a friend both benefitted from cooperating on a task. What was the task? How did you both benefit? What might have happened if you had competed instead?

Letter to Parents

Dear Parents,

In her book *Queen Bees and Wannabees*, Rosalind Wiseman (2009, p.16) points out that "paradoxically, during their greatest period of vulnerability, girls' competition with and judgment of each other weakens their friendships and effectively isolates all of them." Today, in the *Real Friendship* group, the girls participated in a memorable activity designed to demonstrate how cooperation is far more effective than competition in serving the best interests of all of the group members. Ask your daughter to tell you about the *Pull the Rope* game.

Along with learning the value of cooperation, the girls also learned about the importance of empathy in supporting real friendships. Through an activity in which she literally stood in someone else's shoes, your daughter practiced seeing the world from a new perspective and experienced real empathy for an another's point of view.

A fun and engaging at-home activity that you can do with your daughter to reinforce the concept of empathy is to retell a classic fairy tale from a lesser-known point of view. For example, we all know the story of *Jack and the Beanstalk*, but have you ever heard it told from the giant's perspective? Perhaps the giant was not such a villain after all, but rather protective of his family and angry that an intruder had entered his home. Would understanding his point of view create more empathy for his actions? Most children's fairy tales are told from a single point of view and lend themselves well to this type of empathic retelling. Older girls may even enjoy creating a book of rewritten fairy tales.

The animated movies *Hoodwinked* (2006) and *Hoodwinked Too!* (2011) can also provide fun fodder for family-wide discussion about empathy and exploring alternate points of view. The PG-rated kid's films retell the classic fairy tales of *Little Red Riding Hood* and *Hansel and Gretel* from non-traditional perspectives.

If your daughter is mature enough, she may benefit from your guidance with a related concept—that of modifying all-or-nothing thinking. Often, young kids believe that friends must be all good or all bad—their actions completely right or totally wrong. It is difficult for many kids to acknowledge and accept middle-ground perspectives. Use role play to teach your daughter that there are shades of gray to even the most black and white scenarios. Learning to counter all-or-nothing thought traps is an important part of both empathy and flexible thinking.

Session 10

Left Out in the Cold
Understanding the Power of Social Exclusion

Session objectives

- To learn the damaging impact of social exclusion on the group and on individual girls.
- To understand common ways that exclusion is used in social situations among young girls.
- To commit to including others as a basic value of *Real Friendships*.

Materials needed

- 25-piece kid's jigsaw puzzle
- sheets of red, yellow, and green construction (sugar) paper for each girl.

Before beginning

- Prepare the *Exclusion Scenarios* (pages 124 and 125).
- Prepare copies of the *Friendship Journal* (page 126) for each participant.
- Prepare copies of the *Letter to Parents* handout (page 127) for each participant to take home.

Welcome back

1. Welcome girls to the tenth group session.

2. Review last week's session on the values of empathy and cooperation:

   ○ *Who can name the two* Friendship Values *that we talked about last time we met?*

   ○ *Where did you use cooperation this week?*

   ○ *Share an occasion when showing empathy helped a* Real Friendship.

3. Preview this week's agenda:

   ○ *This week, we are going to focus on the value of* Including Others.

   ○ *No one likes to be left out. No one feels good about not being invited. Today, you will get a chance to show your feelings and share your thoughts about typical situations in which this occurs.*

   ○ *As a group, we can commit to the value of* Including Others *and ban the bullying behavior of leaving people out.*

Opening activity: My Piece of the Puzzle

1. For this opening activity, the facilitator will need a 25-piece jigsaw puzzle. Give each girl at least one piece of the puzzle and tell group members that their task is to work together (this is an ideal time to highlight the value of cooperation from the previous session) to assemble the puzzle.

   ○ As an alternative to the 25-piece puzzle, the facilitator can cut up a familiar image from a magazine. Be sure to cut enough pieces so that each group member has at least one piece.

2. Shortly after the group begins, ask 3–4 girls to join you in sitting out of the activity. The girls should not give their puzzle pieces to group members, but rather should retain them, while watching silently from the sidelines. It may be necessary to assure the girls that their exclusion is not a punishment, but rather an important part of the learning activity.

   ○ When selecting group members to sit out, be sure to select enough girls so that the "finished" puzzle will be noticeably incomplete.

   ○ To get the full impact of this activity, the large group will need to be missing at least 6–8 pieces of their puzzle and to have difficulty seeing the final image because of the excluded pieces.

3. Allow the remaining group members to complete what they can of the puzzle. When they are finished, use the following questions to process the activity:

    ◦ *How did it feel to work on the puzzle with so many of your pieces missing?*

    ◦ *How does your puzzle look?*

    ◦ *Does anyone have ideas on why I chose this activity for today?*

4. Summarize the group activity by conveying the following:

    ◦ *We are a group. We do all of our best work and get our best results when all of our members are included.*

    ◦ *Whenever someone is left out, a gaping hole remains.*

    ◦ *When girls intentionally leave other girls out, this is a form of bullying.*

    ◦ *In fact, exclusion* (emphasize this as a new term, if necessary) *is one of the cruelest ways that girls bully each other because it creates feelings of rejection and disconnectedness.*

    ◦ *We are going to spend this session talking about exclusion so that this weapon of bullies is no longer a secret. Whenever you are aware that exclusion is taking place, it is your job to* STANd up *and* Become an Ally *in the situation.*

5. At this point, it is effective to ask the girls who sat on the sidelines to add their pieces to the puzzle, in order to complete the image. Note that it is only when all of the girls are *included* that the task can be complete.

Traffic Lights

The purpose of this activity is to encourage meaningful dialogue among group members about various scenarios related to social exclusion.

1. Give each girl three pieces of colored construction paper—one red, one yellow, and one green—to coordinate with the colors of a traffic light. Explain the activity instructions:

    ◦ *You will listen to a situation read aloud, then hold up the piece of colored paper that coordinates with your thoughts about what has been read.*

    ◦ *If you believe the situation violates* Friendship Values, *hold up the red sheet of paper.*

    ◦ *If you believe the situation was handled well, hold up the green piece of paper.*

    ◦ *If you are not sure or think there is some middle ground on the issue, hold up the yellow piece of paper.*

2. The facilitator should read each *Exclusion Scenario* (from pages 124 and 125) aloud, then facilitate discussion, based on the girls' colored paper selections. Be prepared to ask open-ended, probing questions. Encourage girls to offer meaningful rationales, explanations, and real-life examples for each of their answers.

3. Sample questions for *The Birthday Party* scenario may include:

    ° *What do you think about how Jessie handled the situation?*

    ° *What was wrong with her not inviting Alexa? After all, Alexa did not invite Jessie to her party...*

    ° *If a parent limits the number of invitations that can be extended, how can a girl handle a party guest list, so that no one feels excluded?*

    ° *How do some girls use exclusion as a purposeful way of hurting others?*

    ° *What can you do to* Become an Ally *to a girl(s) who is left out of a party?*

    ° *How would you STANd up to this situation?*

4. Birthday parties are a prime weapon of friendship and tool of social exclusion for young girls. The purpose of discussing this, and other exclusion scenarios, is to bring these normally behind-the-scenes dynamics out into the open and establish a group consensus that this kind of behavior is hurtful to everyone.

5. Use this activity to touch on the finer points of why exclusion occurs (e.g. revenge, anger, power plays, etc.), how it is justified (e.g. "*My mom said I could only invite seven people*"), and what girls can do to withstand exclusion tactics (e.g. *Become an Ally* to the excluded girl, commit to not using exclusion, etc.).

6. Read as many or as few of the *Exclusion Scenarios* as necessary to generate meaningful dialogue and to establish agreement among the girls about how hurtful exclusion can be. The scenarios are written to include "gray areas" about the reasons for exclusion, to encourage critical thinking and discussion among group members about this bullying tactic.

7. Reinforce the idea that as a group, the girls can commit to the value of *Including Others* and agree to ban the bullying behavior of exclusion.

8. Encourage the girls to hold each other accountable, using assertive communication, for the use of social exclusion. It is helpful to bring the activity full circle round, back to the opening puzzle activity, by reminding girls in a visual way that when any one person is left out, the group is less than it could be.

Session conclusion

- *Today, we learned about the painful effects of exclusion on both an individual girl and on the whole group. We brought together many of the skills from previous sessions, in talking about STANding up to exclusion and Becoming an Ally to girls who are left out.*

- *Next week, we will learn a problem solving strategy that girls can use to handle issues like exclusion and other challenges to Real Friendship.*

Friendship Journal

1. Hand out the *Friendship Journal* (page 126).

2. Topic: *Write or draw about a real-life situation in which you or someone you know was left out. How did the person feel? What could she have done in the situation? If you had it to do over again, how would you handle the situation?*

3. The purpose of this assignment is to encourage girls to think about how exclusion shows up in their daily lives and what they can do to handle this commonplace tactic of bullying.

Customizing the curriculum

- Younger kids may need assistance assembling the jigsaw puzzle. Consider using a smaller puzzle or simply cutting a familiar image so that each girl receives one piece.

- It may be helpful to spend additional time explaining the word "exclusion" to younger girls or simply substituting the phrase "leaving girls out."

- The facilitator should determine the relevance of each *Exclusion Scenario* prior to the activity. The scenarios can be edited, omitted and/or replaced with scenarios most relevant to the girls' everyday experiences.

- Older girls may want to use *Exclusion Scenarios* from their real life. As long as no identifiable information is included, allowing girls to write their own scenarios can make the experience more relevant.

Activity: Exclusion Scenarios

Facilitator notes

Select the most relevant scenarios to read aloud to the group, to encourage thoughtful discussion around the topic of social exclusion.

Scenario 1: The Birthday Party

Shortly after school began in the Fall (autumn), Alexa's mother told her she could invite seven friends to her birthday party. Alexa invited her seven best friends from last year's class. Jessie, a new classmate of Alexa's, was not invited to the party. She felt left out, hurt, and angry.

As the school year went on, Alexa and Jessie became friends. They often sat with the same group at lunch and played with the same friends at recess.

In March, Jessie had a birthday party. For weeks, she talked about the party each day in school. She invited all of the girls in her class, except for Alexa.

What do you think about how Jessie handled the situation?

Scenario 2: Pajama Day

As a prize for reading a total of 500 books, Mrs. Hayes allowed all of the kids in her class to wear pajamas to school for a day. When Liza, Kylie, Haley, and Ashleigh all showed up in matching outfits, Emily realized she had been left out of her friends' plan. She wondered why no one told her to wear pink and purple pajamas. She felt embarrassed and left out.

When Emily asked Liza if the four girls planned to match their pajamas, Liza laughed and said, "What do you think?"

When Emily asked Ashleigh why none of the girls included her in the plan, Ashleigh looked at Liza and said, "Oh, sorry Emily. We made a club yesterday and this was just for girls who are in our club."

What do you think about how Liza, Kylie, Haley, and Ashleigh handled the situation?

Scenario 3: Recess Games

A large group of girls are playing Chinese jump rope (skipping) at recess (breaktime). Kristi asks if she can play. Bethany tells Kristi that she can play in the next round.

When the round ends, Bethany hands the rope to Kristi and says, "Here you go!" All of the other girls join Bethany in walking away, leaving Kristi alone with the rope.

What do you think about how Bethany and her friends handled the situation?

Scenario 4: The Sleepover

Madison invited all of her friends to a sleepover. When Chloe found out that she was not invited, her mother called Madison's mother to talk about the party. After the call, Madison's mother insisted that Chloe be invited to the sleepover, emphasizing that it was not okay to leave anyone out.

Madison was angry, but decided it was better to invite Chloe to the sleepover than to have to cancel it altogether. She explained to the other girls why Chloe had to be included.

At the sleepover, the girls paired up to do each other's hair. Chloe was left without a partner.

At dinner, Madison "forgot" to get a drink for Chloe and "accidentally" gave her the last piece of pizza—the one missing half of the cheese.

When the girls went to bed, they laid their sleeping bags together under a blanket fort. There was no room left for Chloe under the fort, so she had to sleep on the sofa.

By midnight, Chloe wished she had never asked to be included in the party.

What do you think about how Madison handled the sleepover?

Scenario 5: The Dance

Leah, Lindsey, and Ava plan to meet at the school dance. When Ava arrives, she can't find Leah and Lindsey anywhere. Thirty minutes after they had planned to meet, Leah and Lindsey show up together. They are wearing matching glow-in-the-dark necklaces. When Ava asks if she can wear one, Leah answers, "Sorry, I don't have any left."

The girls begin to dance together, but after one song, Leah and Lindsey tell Ava that they are going to get a drink. Before Ava can get her money, her friends are gone. She looks for them at the concession stand, but they are nowhere to be found. Finally, she finds them on the dance floor, as partners in the limbo contest.

All night long, Ava finds herself chasing after Leah and Lindsey, who are always together.

What do you think about the way Leah and Lindsey were treating Ava?

✓

Friendship Journal

Write or draw about a real-life situation in which you or someone you know was left out. How did the person feel? What could she have done in the situation? If you had it to do over again, how would you handle the situation?

Letter to Parents

Dear Parents,

Today, in the *Real Friendship* group, your daughter learned about social exclusion. Social exclusion has been identified as the preferred strategy of young girls for expressing anger and "keeping other girls in line" (for example, see *Girlfighting* by Brown 2003). Unfortunately, this tactic of girl bullying is extremely effective for two reasons. First, exclusion plays on the primacy of relationships and connectedness in a young girl's world. Girl bullies rely on threats of exclusion to control their less powerful peers.

Second, social ostracism works because it flies under the radar of most adults; *not* inviting someone to a party or *not* including a girl in a game at recess are distinct from outright, reportable offenses such as hitting, name-calling, or rumor-spreading that adults can observe, see, and hear. Likewise, acts of exclusion can often be easily justified (e.g. *"It's not my fault. My mom said I could only invite five people"*) if they are ever brought to an adult's attention.

Virile in both its intention and its obfuscation, social exclusion creates powerful feelings of rejection and disconnectedness in young people. When it comes to this all-too-common bullying behavior, there are two ways you can help your daughter: first, help her practice skills for coping with being excluded and second, take a firm stand against her initiating this behavior.

Ask your daughter to tell you about the group's *My Piece of the Puzzle* activity. Encourage her to describe why inclusion is critical to a group's success. Also, encourage your daughter to share examples of the *Traffic Lights* activity. In this group discussion the girls shared their thoughts and experiences about typical social situations in which exclusion is used as a tool to exact revenge, express anger, and exert power. The purpose of the *Traffic Lights* activity was to bring behind-the-scenes dynamics out into the open and to establish a group consensus that exclusionary behavior is hurtful to everyone.

At home, talk with your daughter about how she sees exclusion used among her peers. Be aware that for young girls, birthday parties can be a prime weapon of exclusion. When planning your child's parties, play dates, sleepovers, and other special events, consider what you can do to ensure that guest lists are not misused.

It is also helpful to use discussion and role play to help your daughter prepare for how she can respond if she is the target of exclusion. Many of the skills she has learned thus far in group are helpful in countering exclusion, including STANding up for herself, drawing upon her personal strengths, and reaching out to connect with supportive friends.

Sharing SODAS
A Problem Solving Method for Girls

Session objectives

- To learn a five-step problem solving method for handling conflict.
- To practice the SODAS problem solving strategy using role play.

Materials needed

- flipchart paper and markers
- unlined paper for each participant
- pencils, crayons, and markers for each participant
- hard surface for girls to complete drawing task.

Before beginning

- Pre-print flipchart paper with the SODAS acronym:
  - **S**ituations
  - **O**ptions
  - **D**isadvantages
  - **A**dvantages
  - **S**olutions.
- Prepare copies of *SODAS Scenarios* (page 135) for each group member.
- Prepare copies of the *Friendship Journal* (page 136) for each participant.
- Prepare copies of the *Letter to Parents* handout (page 137) for each participant to take home.

Welcome back

1. Welcome girls to the eleventh session. Remind girls that next week will be the final session of the group. Emphasize the significant learning that has taken place up to this point and the *Real Friendship* bonds that have been formed.

2. Review last week's session on social exclusion:

    ○ *Did you observe or experience any incidents of exclusion among girls this week?*

    ○ *What happened?*

    ○ *How did you STANd up for yourself in the incident?*

    ○ *How did you act like an ally to the girl who was excluded?*

    ○ If an example of exclusion is shared, consider using it to show the group how to work through the SODAS method below.

3. Preview this week's agenda:

    ○ *Bullying is a real problem for young girls. When bullying is disguised as friendship, the problems become even more complex and confusing.*

    ○ *The* SODAS Problem Solving Method *gives you an easy-to-remember way to go about solving all sorts of challenging friendship situations.*

Opening activity: SODAS Problem Solving Method

1. On pre-printed flipchart paper, reveal the SODAS acronym to the girls:

    ○ **S**ituation

    ○ **O**ptions

    ○ **D**isadvantages

    ○ **A**dvantages

    ○ **S**olutions.

2. Use a real-world scenario to walk girls through each step of the *SODAS Problem Solving Method*. A sample scenario is provided below, though facilitators may substitute in their own example or allow a group member to suggest a problem.

Please note: This scenario is written to show how a parent helps a child through the SODAS process. Once kids know how to use SODAS, they are often able to work through the process with a trustworthy friend (ally) or even independently.

Scenario

Jenna came home from school on Friday in tears—again! She seemed sad and frustrated every afternoon this week, but she didn't want to tell anyone why. I decided it was a good time to help her tackle whatever was bugging her. I started by asking her to tell me what was making her feel so upset.

- **S**ituation

  Move beyond the emotion of the moment and identify what it is about a specific situation that is causing a problem.

  Jenna: *Abby wouldn't talk to me after recess today because she was mad that I played with Hailey. Hailey tells me I'm not her friend anymore every time I sit with Abby on the bus. I like both girls but it makes me so frustrated to be pulled between them!*

  Jenna identified the problem situation. Next, her mother asked her to consider her options.

- **O**ptions

  Practice brainstorming skills. At this point in the process, a child should be encouraged to creatively list all of the options for solving the problem. Don't put limits on the free-flowing process.

  - *I could just try to ignore Abby and Hailey when they are being mean to me.*

  - *I could eat lunch with Abby and play with Hailey at recess.*

  - *I could talk to both girls and explain that I like them both and want to find a way to all get along.*

  - *I could tell them both to just leave me alone.*

  Jenna wrote her ideas down on a piece of paper as they came to her. There was no editing at this early stage—just brainstorming all the options for her social dilemma.

- **D**isadvantages

  Here's where the editing comes in. After all of the options have been generated, show girls how to consider the potential negative or unintended consequences of the various options.

This step is where it is especially helpful to work with a partner. Parents, friends, and those not directly involved in the situation often provide "cooler heads" to think through the disadvantages and advantages of options. For example, Jenna's mother might ask helpful questions like:

○ *What might be the disadvantages of ignoring the girls?*

○ *Is there a downside to trying to divide your time?*

○ *What is the worst thing that could happen if you talked honestly to Abby and Hailey about the problem?*

○ *What are the risks of ending the friendships altogether?*

Jenna's mom encourages her daughter to consider each option by asking non-leading questions about the disadvantages of each.

• **A**dvantages

This step is the flip-side of the previous one. Jenna is now encouraged to consider the advantages of each option.

○ *What good could come if you ignored Abby and Hailey?*

○ *How might dividing your time be helpful?*

○ *How could talking honestly to both girls improve your friendships?*

○ *How could ending the friendships improve your situation?*

• **S**olution

In this final step, girls weigh the advantages and disadvantages of each option and select the solution that they believe can be most effective. It is often helpful to help girls generate plans A and B, for challenging friendship problems. Likewise, role-playing several possible solutions is often the best way for girls to learn about potential outcomes and practice effective responses.

Jenna: *I think I'm going to try telling both Abby and Hailey that they mean a lot to me as friends and that it is important to me to be able to spend time with more than one friend in school each day. I'll even see if the three of us can use SODAS to figure out a way that we can all enjoy spending time together.*

Sometimes the best questions for a child to ask herself are, "*What do I want to have happen in this situation?*" and "*Is this a solution I can live with?*"

SODAS Scenarios

1. Once the *SODAS Problem Solving Method* has been reviewed and you feel confident that the girls understand the process, allow them the opportunity to work through a few scenarios.

2. Arrange the girls in small groups of 3–4. Give each girl a *SODAS Scenarios* activity sheet. Provide each group with a large piece of flipchart paper (spread out on a table or taped to a wall) to record the process. Tell the girls that their goal is to generate 1–2 effective Solutions and to be prepared to role play the solution for the group.

3. The facilitator can provide assistance as necessary, but allow the girls enough freedom to work through the process. Some of the best learning comes from mistakes and from group feedback.

4. Allow approximately ten minutes for the groups to work through the SODAS process, then invite the groups to come back together.

5. Give each group the opportunity to present their scenario and their SODAS process. Allow for feedback, questions, and comments along the way.

6. Encourage each group to role play one chosen solution. Affirm each group's efforts and ask for other participants to discuss their thoughts on how the SODAS method was used for the problem scenario. This is a great time for girls to share similar real-life experiences and the kinds of solutions they have chosen in the past.

7. After each small group has had the opportunity to share their role play, wrap up the discussion by affirming that girls who are equipped with reliable problem solving skills benefit from the confidence of knowing that they can handle any problem that comes along.

Session conclusion

- *This week, we learned the* SODAS Problem Solving Method *and practiced using the method to work through friendship dilemmas. Early on, you may want to work with a partner or parent to use SODAS, but, before you know it, you will be able to use the five steps all on your own to solve problems.*

- *Next week will be our final group session. We will pull together all of the things we have learned in the* Real Friendship *group and become authors of our own books.*

Friendship Journal

1. Hand out the *Friendship Journal* (page 136).

2. Topic: *Think about a problem situation you have experienced with a friend. Use the SODAS method to describe the **S**ituation, brainstorm **O**ptions, evaluate their **D**isadvantages and **A**dvantages, and then choose the best **S**olution.*

3. The purpose of this activity is to give the girls practice working through the SODAS method outside of the group.

Customizing the curriculum

- Younger children may benefit from an explanation of each of the SODAS terms. For example, it may be helpful to further define an "option" as a "choice." As you explain each step of the process, be sure to modify the language as necessary.

- As you teach the SODAS method, use the provided scenario or create a customized one to match the experiences and abilities of your participants.

- Younger participants may need a greater amount of support from the facilitator in brainstorming options and evaluating disadvantages and advantages. Instead of working in small groups, consider working through an additional example as a large group.

- Older participants may catch on to the SODAS process quickly. Allow older girls to create their own real-world friendship problems (being careful not to include identifiable information) and work through them at their own pace.

Activity: SODAS Scenarios

Scenario 1

Molly and Mia are planning a sleepover for Mia's birthday. Sophia overhears the girls talking and asks if she can be invited too. Mia's mom told her that she could only invite one friend to sleep over, but Mia doesn't want to make Sophia feel left out.

Scenario 2

Nicole and Katie have been best friends since kindergarten. They take dance lessons together and love to put on shows for their parents. When Jodi moves in next door to Nicole, Nicole starts to want to play with her every day after school. Nicole and Jodi both like to ride bikes. Katie doesn't even have a bicycle. Katie feels left out and angry at Nicole.

Scenario 3

Addison's mother packs her favorite kind of cookie in her lunch. As soon as Addison opens her lunch bag, Grace and Taylor see the cookies and each ask if they can have one. Since Addison only has two cookies, she doesn't know what to do.

Scenario 4

Lily whispers to Ella about how ugly Samantha's outfit looks. Ella agrees that she doesn't like Samantha's clothing, but knows that it's not kind to make fun of other people. She laughs anyway, because she doesn't want Lily to be mad at her. Later that day, Lily writes Ella a note, telling her that Samantha is too poor to buy new clothes. The note tells Ella to "pass it on" to the other girls in the class. Ella is worried that if she stands up to Lily, Lily will spread rumors about her next.

✓

Friendship Journal

Think about a problem situation you have experienced with a friend. Use the SODAS method to describe the **S**ituation, brainstorm **O**ptions, evaluate their **D**isadvantages and **A**dvantages, and then choose the best **S**olution.

Letter to Parents

Dear Parents,

Today, in the *Real Friendship* group, your daughter learned a simple but highly effective problem solving strategy. SODAS is an easy-to-remember method that allows girls to work through challenging friendship dilemmas and come up with helpful solutions. Ask your daughter to explain the acronym to you and talk about each of the five steps.

At first, your daughter will benefit from your assistance in brainstorming options and evaluating their potential effectiveness. In no time, however, she will be able to work her own way through friendship challenges and will likely be able to apply SODAS to all types of problems in her life.

Encourage your daughter to apply SODAS often, so that the process becomes second nature. Role play various possible outcomes, to help her become well versed in selecting the best possible solutions. Remind her that even if a chosen solution does not bring about a desired outcome, the process was not a failure; simply encourage her to always be prepared with Plans B and C and to approach any situation as a problem that can be solved.

Writing How-To Books
Ending the Group, Maintaining the Bonds

Session objectives

- To reflect on the knowledge and skills gained during the group sessions and create "How-To" books to share individual learning.

- To gain a sense of personal accomplishment in completing the *Real Friendship* group.

- To commit to using *Real Friendship* behaviors beyond the scope of the group.

Materials needed

- flipchart paper and markers

- journal or lined paper for each participant

- pencils, pens, crayons, or markers for each participant

- *Real Friendship Pledges*

- *Certificates of Achievement*

- *Participant Evaluation Forms.*

Before beginning

- Prepare copies of the *Participant Evaluation Form* (page 146) for each participant.

- Prepare copies of the *Real Friendship Pledge* (page 144 for younger girls; page 145 for older girls) for each participant.

- Prepare copies of the *Certificate of Achievement* (page 147), personalized with each group member's name.

- Prepare copies of the *Letter to Parents* handout (page 148) for each participant to take home.

Welcome back

1. Welcome girls to the final group session.

2. Review last week's session on the *SODAS Problem Solving Method*. Ask girls to talk about any occasions over the past week that they have had to work through a problem, using SODAS.

3. Preview this week's agenda:

   ° *This is our final session of the* Real Friendship *group. Together, you have learned and accomplished so much.*

   ° *Although the group meetings will be coming to an end, the caring and supportive bonds you have formed can last forever.*

   ° *It will be up to you now to practice all of the skills you have learned. Remind each other how important it is to stay true to* Real Friendship Values *and to always STANd up to bullying behavior.*

   ° *Today, we are going to do one last activity to help you pull together all of your new knowledge and skills.*

How-To Books

In this final group activity, the girls will have the opportunity to become authors, as they create manuals to teach new *Real Friendship* group participants "How-To" skills for coping with bullying behavior.

This creative activity allows participants to gain a sense of competence as they become teachers for a next group of girls, while at the same time giving them the opportunity to integrate their new knowledge and skills into a written keepsake.

Be sure to allow enough time at the end of the session for a book reading by each author.

1. Provide each girl with a journal-sized notebook or several sheets of lined writing paper, along with a pencil or pen and the following instructions:

- ○ *People who write books are usually experts in their field. After all of your hard work and participation in this group, you are an expert in knowing how to recognize and respond to bullying behavior. So today, you will become an author.*

- ○ *Your job in this last group session is to write a* How-To Book. *A* How-To Book *is like an instruction manual that gives readers step-by-step skills for how to do something.*

- ○ *Imagine that next month, I will be meeting with a group of girls who have never attended a* Real Friendship *group. These girls might not even know that gossiping and leaving people out count as bullying behaviors. They probably have no idea how to show strength or assert themselves. I'll bet they wouldn't know how to be an ally to a friend.*

- ○ *These girls need instructions and you are just the expert to help them.*

- ○ *Using your new Journals (or lined paper), begin to write a* How-To Book, *to share your new knowledge and skills for coping with bullying behavior.*

- ○ *Be as creative and expressive as you want to be. Your book can include words, illustrations, lists, or even ideas for games and activities.*

- ○ *Before we end the group today, you each will have the chance to read or share a page from your book with the rest of the group.*

2. Allow time for the girls to create their *How-To Books.* Save at least 20 minutes at the end of the group session to allow each girl to share a page from her manual and complete the closing activities.

3. Encourage each girl to select a page from her *How-To Book* and share it with the group. Affirm each presentation and thank each girl individually for her contributions to the *Real Friendship* group.

4. It is unlikely that most girls will have the opportunity to complete their *How-To Book* before the group ends. Encourage the girls to take their Journals home with them and continue to write their manuals after the group has ended.

5. Let the girls know that as they have new experiences, they will learn even more about how to handle bullying behavior. Each time they learn a new skill or lesson, this knowledge can be recorded in their *How-To Book.* Perhaps they may become published authors one day, and share all that they have learned about bullying with girls from all over the world!

Real Friendship Pledges

It is always helpful to close groups with an acknowledgement of each participant's accomplishments and personal contributions to the group experience. Writing *How-To Books* is one powerful way for the girls to gain a sense of their overall learning and to create a keepsake of their new knowledge and skills.

The closing activity of the group should also include two additional mementos: the signing of a *Real Friendship Pledge* (page 144 or 145) and a *Certificate of Achievement* (page 147).

1. Hand out a copy of the *Real Friendship Pledge* to each girl.

2. Ask for several volunteers to take turns reading sections of the *Pledge* aloud. Then, ask each girl to sign the *Pledge*.

3. Encourage the girls to keep the pledge with them on a daily basis—in a school folder, backpack, or other spot where they can see it daily and remind themselves regularly of their commitment to *STANd up to Bullying* whenever and wherever they see it.

Participant Evaluation Form

1. Hand each girl a brief *Participant Evaluation Form* (page 146). While girls at this age may have difficulty giving detailed feedback about their group experience, allowing them the opportunity to share their feelings in a meaningful way is an important acknowledgment of their opinions.

2. Emphasize to girls that their feedback about the group experience is important. Ask each participant to complete the *Evaluation Form* and turn it in when they receive their *Certificate*.

Session conclusion and Certificate of Achievement

1. Give the girls a sincere thank-you for their active participation in the group sessions and a heartfelt acknowledgement of their learning. It is meaningful to make direct eye contact with each girl as you affirm their experiences in the *Real Friendship* group.

2. Call each girl to the front of the group room to receive a *Certificate of Achievement*. As the girls are receiving their certificate, offer a few personalized words about each girl, to acknowledge their unique contributions to the group.

3. When each Certificate has been handed out, wish each girl success in their friendships. If relevant, let the girls know that you remain available as a supportive and trustworthy adult whenever they need to talk about *Real Friendship*.

Customizing the curriculum

- Younger participants can be encouraged to create a picture book to share their *How-To* knowledge, while older participants are encouraged to use words to write about their new knowledge and skills.

- Two versions of a *Real Friendship Pledge* are included. One includes simpler vocabulary and phrasing for younger group members while the second is designed for older participants who can comprehend at a higher level. Choose the version of the pledge that is appropriate for your group participants.

- It is important for all group members to have the opportunity to provide their feedback on the *Real Friendship* group experience. The facilitator should offer assistance, as necessary, to younger participants who may lack experience or skills completing *Evaluation Forms*.

✓

Real Friendship Pledge

In this group, I learned about being a real friend to others. I promise to be an ally to girls and to help stop bullying behavior whenever I see it.

By signing this pledge, I will:

1. Do my best to live according to *Real Friendship Values*.

2. Use *Builders* to show kindness.

3. *STANd up* for myself and others.

4. Act like an *Ally*.

5. Feel proud of my own personal strengths.

6. Connect with others.

7. Cooperate with others.

8. Show empathy.

9. Include others.

10. Use SODAS to solve problems.

I will talk to an adult whenever I see bullying going on.

If I ever act like a bully, I know that others will tell an adult about it.

Name: _____ Date: _____

Real Friendship Pledge

As a member of the *Real Friendships* group, I learned all about *Friendship Values* that build girls up as well as about bullying behaviors that tear girls down. Even though the group is ending, I commit to using my new knowledge and skills to be an ally to girls and to help put an end to bullying behavior whenever I see it.

By signing this pledge, I promise to:

1. Do my best to live according to *Real Friendship Values*.

2. Use *Builders* to show kindness and build others' self-esteem.

3. *STANd up* for myself and others whenever bullying is occurring.

4. Act like an *Ally* before, during, and after bullying occurs.

5. Feel proud of my own personal strengths.

6. Connect with others—both people who are similar to me and those who are different.

7. Cooperate with others to reach group goals.

8. Show empathy for other people's points of view.

9. Include others whenever possible.

10. Solve problems and confront conflict directly and assertively.

Whenever I am aware of bullying behavior, I will talk about it right away with a trustworthy adult. I also understand that if I am bullying someone, other people have the responsibility of reporting my behavior to an adult.

Name: _____   Date: _____

Real Friendship Group: Participant Evaluation Form

What did you like best about this group?

Was there a specific activity or discussion that you thought was really good?

What could be done to improve this group?

What is the most important thing you learned in this group?

Name (optional): _____

This certificate is proudly presented to

_____

for completing the

Real Friendship

group

_____

Facilitator's name

_____

Date

Letter to Parents

Dear Parents,

Today marked the final session of the *Real Friendship* group. To celebrate your daughter's achievement and honor her expertise, we commissioned her to write her own *How-To* manual, to teach others how to recognize and respond effectively to bullying disguised as friendship. Ask her to show you her work-in-progress and share with you a completed chapter. She may even be up for a book signing! Encourage her to finish her *How-To* manual at home, as a way to integrate her new knowledge and skills into a written keepsake.

Though the group sessions have come to an end, it is our hope that your daughter continues to hone her skills for coping with bullying and that the bonds she formed with fellow group members endure. To that end, your daughter signed a *Real Friendship Pledge* to commit to practicing the skills she learned in group. She also received a *Certificate of Achievement*, to honor her hard work and significant learning. Encourage her to post or frame the *Pledge* and *Certificate* in highly visible locations, to remind herself often of her commitment to *Real Friendship*.

Thank you for all of your support and encouragement of your daughter throughout this group experience. No child should have to navigate the choppy and often-confusing waters of friendship alone. Working together, parents and professionals are in the best position to create safe and open forums in which girls can talk, learn, compare experiences, and gain lifelong skills for asserting themselves when confronted with incidents of cruelty disguised as friendship.

Supplementary Activities

Preparing Girls for a Social Media World

The activities and discussions described in this section are designed to guide girls who have begun to explore and consume the social media worlds of texting, Facebook, song lyrics, music videos, and advertising.

While younger girls may not yet own their own cell phones or have (legal/ sanctioned) access to a Facebook account, chances are excellent that they know someone who does and are quite familiar with the hows and whys of social media use. For older girls, it is almost a certainty that they have browsed YouTube at least a time or two and have seen and heard age-inappropriate content in fashion magazines and music lyrics. By the early school years, young girls are inundated with content that most adults would agree does not serve their best interests.

As there is no escape from the social media world and no use denying its impact on young girls, it is important for helping adults to teach girls how to think critically about ubiquitous media messages and how to use technology in ways that contribute to the development of *Real Friendships*.

Because the activities and discussions around social media will vary so much by age group (e.g. conversations about music lyrics may be applicable to girls of all ages but ground rules for texting and cell phone use may only be readily applicable to older girls) the activities that follow are provided as a supplement to the *Friendship and Other Weapons* curriculum, rather than as a part of the regular 12-week program. Three distinct topic areas focus on song lyrics and YouTube video content, advertising images and self-esteem, and guidelines for texting and social media use. The Supplementary Activities may be incorporated into the regular 12-session curriculum or used separately, on an as-needed basis.

Supplementary activity objectives

- To teach girls how to think critically about ubiquitous media messages.

- To learn how to use technology in ways that contribute to the development of *Real Friendships*.

Supplementary Session 1
Tame that Tune
Evaluating Music Lyrics and Video Imagery

Session objective

- To examine the messages of popular song lyrics and video imagery.

Materials needed

- flipchart paper and markers
- CD or MP3 player, with speakers
- (optional) Internet connection for viewing YouTube video selection.

Before beginning

- Prepare copies of the *Friendship Journal* (page 156) for each participant.
- Prepare copies of the *Letter to Parents* handout (page 157) for each participant to take home.

Please note that this session will require advanced preparation and planning. Participants are asked to bring in an example of one of their favorite songs, either on a CD or downloaded onto an MP3 player. This task should be given as a "homework" assignment prior to the scheduled session, so that participants have time to make their music selection. The *Letter to Parents* (on page 157) should be given prior to the session, at the same time that the "homework" is explained to the girls, rather than after the session, as is customary.

Also, it will be critical that the facilitator thoroughly reviews the song and lyric selections of the girls prior to playing any of them for the large group. As this can be time-consuming, the facilitator should ask that the girls bring in their song selections at least two days prior to the scheduled session.

Welcome back

1. Welcome the girls to the session.

2. Review the previous week's session.

3. Preview this week's activities:

    ° *Music is important in the lives of young people, but what does it have to do with bullying or making* Real Friendships*?* (Allow volunteers to respond, affirming all answers.)

    ° *Most of us are drawn to songs because of their catchy music or because we like the singer or band. We may find ourselves singing along quietly—or even at the top of our lungs—but how often do we really think about the words we are repeating?*

    ° *This week, we are going to take a look at popular song lyrics and images from music videos as a way of understanding how music and video messages influence how we think about ourselves and feel about others.*

    ° *When we are aware of the negative messages we take in—whether from music, video, or even bullying—we are better prepared to withstand its influence.*

Tame that Tune: Evaluating Music Lyrics and Video Imagery

Messages embedded in song lyrics and video imagery influence the ways girls think about themselves and their relationships with others. The purpose of this activity is to help participants become aware of media messages that violate values and degrade girls, as these messages can make girls more vulnerable to negative, "shredding" messages from bullies.

1. As a "homework" assignment prior to this session, challenge girls to bring in an example of one of their favorite songs, either on a CD or downloaded onto an MP3 player.

    ° If time permits and the technology is available, girls may also be invited to suggest favorite YouTube videos.

2. To start the activity, convey the widespread appeal of music:

    ° *Music is universal in almost every culture and across all age groups, around the world, throughout much of history. Human beings just love music!*

3. Ask questions to generate discussion, such as:

    ○ *What is it that you like about music?*

    ○ *Does the music you like have lyrics?*

    ○ *Do you pay attention to the lyrics?*

    ○ *Have you ever found yourself singing lyrics, even when you are not sure what they mean?*

    ○ *Have you ever seen an adult cringe when they hear the lyrics to one of your favorite songs? Which ones? Why do you think they cringe at the lyrics?*

4. Select a few examples of the songs that group members brought to the session.

    ○ Please note: While *Letters to Parents* are usually sent after the group sessions, a pre-session letter is provided for this Supplementary Activity so that the facilitator can notify parents that participants will be examining popular music lyrics and YouTube video clips. *When necessary, secure permission from parents before doing this activity.*

    ○ Select lyrics and videos that will teach girls about the potential negative impact of media messages without exposing them to content that is over-the-top offensive and/or explicit. While the purpose of this activity is to increase young girls' awareness of messages embedded in music lyrics and video imagery, the activity is not intended to expose girls to explicit content within the group setting. *Use caution when selecting the music or videos to play in the group.*

5. Begin with a focus on popular music. Play a selected song at a comfortable volume, so that girls can discern song lyrics. After the song has played once (or twice, if necessary), ask the girls to talk about the lyrics:

    ○ *How did you feel when you listened to this song?*

    ○ *What is this song about?*

    ○ *Were there any words that you didn't understand?*

    ○ *Have you ever watched the music video for this song?*

    ○ *Did the video storyline match the words?*

    ○ *How did the video make you feel when you watched it?*

    ○ *How were the actors/dancers in the video dressed?*

6. If a YouTube clip is to be used, this is a good time to add video imagery to the discussion.

7. Repeat the activity with examples of several different songs and/or videos.

8. There is almost limitless potential for talking about pop music and videos of the day, from lead singers to their fashions, to the messages they are trying to convey, and so on. The facilitator should attend to the interests of their group, encouraging discussion around the theme of media messages and how destructive and degrading messages are sometimes hidden within songs and videos.

9. The takeaway point of this activity should not be to condemn music and videos or even to dampen a girl's enthusiasm for them. Rather, asking girls to evaluate music lyrics and video imagery can help them become more informed consumers and critical thinkers about any and all of the influences of technology and media that surround them on a daily basis.

10. When girls learn to ask themselves questions about what they are hearing, seeing, dancing to day after day, and singing out loud, they develop a protective measure of insight and control over ubiquitous media messages—rather than the other way around.

Session conclusion

- *Today, we talked about how the messages in popular songs and music videos influence how we think about ourselves and feel about others.*

- *We learned that it is important for girls to be aware of media messages that put girls down, since these messages can make girls more vulnerable to the kind of bullying behavior that also "shreds" a girl's self-image.*

Friendship Journal

1. Hand out the *Friendship Journal* (page 156) to each participant.

2. Topic: *Write an original song, with lyrics that reflect the values that are important to you.*

3. For girls ages 8–11, the facilitator may choose to add this topic: *If you have the chance to work with a group this week, create a two-minute skit, as a mock up of a YouTube video.*

4. The purpose of this activity is to encourage girls to think about replacing negative media messages with more positive, image-enhancing ones.

Customizing the curriculum

- The facilitator should use care in determining the songs to be played aloud in group and the lyrics to be discussed. Even within a single-age group, participants may have a wide range of experience and exposure to song lyrics and music video imagery—from no exposure at all to great familiarity—depending on family choices, living with an older sibling, etc.

- While the objective of the activity remains to help group participants become more informed consumers and critical thinkers about music and video influences, it is also important to keep the content age-appropriate.

- For the youngest participants, session content can be limited to evaluating song lyrics.

- It is suggested to reserve any evaluation of video imagery for older participants, in the 8–11-year-old range.

✓

Friendship Journal

Write an original song, with lyrics that reflect the values that are important to you.

Letter to Parents

Dear Parents,

Ordinarily, I send you a letter after your daughter's *Real Friendship* group session. This week, the group will be doing something different, however, so I want to tell you about it ahead of time and ask for your permission to let your daughter participate in a unique way.

In our upcoming session, the girls will be learning to think about the messages contained in popular music and video. Your daughter is invited to bring in an example of one of her favorite songs, either on a CD or downloaded onto an MP3 player. If time permits, we may also look at popular music videos commonly viewed by girls your daughter's age.

Messages embedded in song lyrics and video imagery influence the ways girls think about themselves and their relationships with others. The purpose of this activity is to help participants become aware of media messages that violate values and degrade girls, as these messages can make girls more vulnerable to negative messages from bullies. The intention is not to expose girls to explicit content. Discretion will be used in selecting the songs and videos to be shared.

With your permission, please allow your daughter to select a song or video to share with the group. Both before and after the *Real Friendship* group session, please engage her in a discussion about the meaning of selected song lyrics and/or video images. Many websites enable users to download song lyrics. This is a great at-home activity for parents and kids to practice the skills of critical thinking about media messages and evaluation of how those messages interplay with personal values. Encouraging dialogue about media messages is an effective way that parents can help their daughters become active thinkers about media messages rather than passive, vulnerable consumers.

Is Seeing Really Believing?
Evaluating Entertainment and Advertising Imagery

Session objective

- To think critically about entertainment and advertising imagery.

Materials needed

- examples of before/after airbrushing celebrity photos (available on the internet)
- copy of the film *Dove Evolution* for viewing by participants
- (optional) copy of the film *Beauty Pressure* for viewing by participants.

Before beginning

- Prepare copies of the *Friendship Journal* (page 165) for each participant.
- Prepare copies of the *Letter to Parents* handout (page 166) for each participant to take home.

Welcome back

1. Welcome the girls to the session.

2. Review the previous week's session.

3. Preview this week's session:

   ○ *Raise your hand if you have ever:*

- *watched television*

- *paid attention to an advertisement*

- *looked at a magazine*

- *seen a picture of a model.*

  ○ *This week, we are going to take a look at how popular advertisements and photos of celebrities bend the truth and trick us into seeing things that do not really exist.*

  ○ *When we understand the false nature of entertainment and advertising messages, we are better able to feel good about our true selves. As we know from our session about realizing personal strengths, when we feel good about ourselves, it is harder for a bully—or an advertisement—to make us feel badly.*

Is Seeing Really Believing? Resisting the Pressure of Impossible Standards

This session is designed to encourage girls to think critically about the messages sent through entertainment and advertising. It can be used independently or as a partner to the activity about song lyrics in Session I. Both are useful in helping kids realize that unrealistic portrayals of girls and women are woven into their daily lives. When girls are aware of how entertainment and advertising images are altered, they are better able to resist the pressures of "measuring up" to the images.

1. In preparation for the activity, ask the girls:

   ○ *Is seeing really believing?*

2. Convey to the girls that the images that are portrayed in entertainment and advertising do not necessarily reflect the lives of actual people. Nor, in fact, are many of the images we see even real.

3. Ask girls if they are familiar with the term "airbrushing." Explain the concept, to demonstrate that images in the media trick girls into believing that "perfection" exists. Emphasize that when girls take in these messages without questioning them, they can begin to feel bad about themselves, worrying that they don't measure up to impossible standards.

4. Several examples of airbrushing and before/after comparisons of celebrity photos are available on the internet. It may be helpful for the facilitator to have examples on hand to show to participants.

5. Among the best examples for use with young girls is a video called *Dove Evolution*. This video is available on YouTube or by typing "Dove Campaign for Real Beauty" into an online search engine. This brief video clip shows the transformation of an everyday-looking woman into a billboard-ready supermodel. It is a great discussion tool for showing young girls how it takes an army of professionals to transform one model and that even with the large team of hair and make-up artists, the model still needs digital alteration before her image is projected to the world.

6. Show participants the video, instructing them to look carefully at all of the work that goes into preparing a model for a photo shoot. Because the images flash by quickly, it is often helpful to show the video more than once.

7. After showing girls this video, remind them that *seeing should never be believing* when it comes to images in the media.

8. This is often an eye-opening video for girls who, even at a young age, are already major consumers of media messages. The facilitator should attend to the specific questions and comments of group members and encourage discussion about how the media creates images that are unattainable in real life.

9. The takeaway point of this activity is to encourage girls to feel good about exactly who they are and not to compare themselves to media images that are neither real nor attainable (without a team of professionals and digital alteration).

10. As with the previous activity about music lyrics, this session encourages girls to think critically about media images and to become informed consumers rather than passive recipients of the media.

Virtual Shopping

1. Emphasize to participants that airbrushed imagery in entertainment and advertising is not limited to adult audiences. Kids are the target market for unrealistic products of all kinds, every day.

2. Prior to the group session, collect toy catalogs from popular stores.

3. Arrange participants in pairs or small groups. Give each group 1–2 catalogs, along with a piece of paper and pen, and explain this assignment:

- *Browse through the catalog at the types of toys, games, and activities available for kids your age.*

- *With your partner or small group, talk about which items represent "real" girls engaged in realistic activities vs. which show girls in unrealistic outfits, wearing adult make-up, or doing things you couldn't imagine a girl your age doing.*

- *On a piece of paper, tally the number of items that represent "real" girls in one column. In a second column, tally the number of products that represent unrealistic products for kids your age.*

4. Allow approximately 10 minutes for the girls to work together to browse the catalog images, then bring the participants back for a large group discussion:

- *What kinds of images and products stood out for you as you were browsing the catalogs?*

- *Did you find more realistic items that represent the look and real-life activities of girls your age, or more unrealistic ones? How do you explain your findings?*

- *Is this something you have ever thought about before as you looked through store catalogs or browsed in store aisles?*

  - Explain that most consumers never stop to think about the kinds of products being offered or the impact of what is advertised by stores.

- *How can becoming a critical thinker about the products advertised for children help you to resist the pressures of unrealistic imagery? How will you withstand media influences and hold on to feeling good about your realistic self?*

Session conclusion

- *Today, we talked about how the images in entertainment and advertising can impact how we think about ourselves and feel about others. We also learned that many of these images are airbrushed, altered, and completely unrealistic.*

- *Seeing should never be believing when it comes to the images in the media.*

- *No one is perfect. Trying to live up to perfect standards just makes us feel badly about ourselves.*

- *Instead, our goal should be to focus on our strengths and to feel good about exactly who we are. Bullies—and advertisers—will have a hard time getting us down when we are aware of their negative messages and strong enough to replace them with positive messages of our own.*

Friendship Journal

1. Hand out the *Friendship Journal* (page 165).

2. Explain to girls that many organizations and media outlets do make efforts to produce content that encourages girls to feel good about their real, un-airbrushed selves. Part of their *Friendship Journal* topic for the week will be researching such organizations and publications.

3. It may be helpful to provide examples of organizations and publications that support "real" girls and aim to build positive self-esteem in young people, including:

   ◦ The World Association of Girl Guides and Girl Scouts (www. wagggsworld.org)

   ◦ Girls on the Run (www.girlsontherun.org)

   ◦ New Moon Girls (www.newmoongirls.com)

   ◦ The Kind Campaign (www.kindcampaign.com).

4. Topic: *This week, pay attention to images of girls and women in the media, but do so with a critical eye, keeping in the front of your mind how these images are altered to create unreal standards of beauty and degrading ideas about the roles of women. Do your own research to find programs, publications, and images that provide you with more realistic and inspiring messages. Rather than writing or drawing, share these examples as part of your Journal.*

5. The purpose of this activity is to teach girls where to look for positive, inspiring organizations and media messages.

Customizing the curriculum

• If time permits, a second video from the Dove Campaign for Real Beauty, called *Beauty Pressure* can be useful in teaching girls positive messages about self-esteem. The clip emphasizes how the media inflicts pressure on girls to be "younger, smaller, firmer and tighter." Because the message is more complex than the *Dove Evolution* film, this clip may be best suited for girls ages 8–11. This film has also been titled *Dove—onslaught*.

- For older girls, it may be helpful to use fashion and entertainment industry magazines in place of toy catalogs. Participants can be asked to compare the number of realistic images of girls vs. those that appear airbrushed and altered. A second topic for comparison can be to tally the number of advertisements that feature girls to sell hair, make-up, or beauty products vs. those that show girls engaged in activities that emphasize their intelligence and abilities.

Friendship Journal

This week, pay attention to images of girls and women in the media, but do so with a critical eye, keeping in the front of your mind how these images are altered to create unreal standards of beauty and degrading ideas about the roles of women.

Do your own research to find programs and publications that provide girls with realistic images and inspiring messages. Rather than writing or drawing, share these examples as part of your Journal.

Letter to Parents

Dear Parents,

Today, in the *Real Friendship* group, your daughter learned that images portrayed in entertainment and advertising do not necessarily reflect the real lives of real people. The girls watched a brief film called *Dove Evolution* to see first-hand how media images are altered and young girls are misled to believe that perfection exists. The purpose of today's activity and discussion was to encourage girls to feel good about exactly who they are and not to allow themselves to be vulnerable to negative messages—whether they come from entertainment sources or from "friends."

Your daughter also went on a "virtual" shopping trip in group, browsing through catalogs and magazines. She talked about the types of products that are commonly marketed to kids her age and discussed which items represent "real" girls vs. which show girls in age-inappropriate outfits, wearing adult make-up, or involved in activities that are hardly kid-oriented.

This week, spend some time with your daughter, browsing through popular entertainment, fashion, and even news magazines with your daughter. Keep a count of the number of images that show girls or women advertising a hair or beauty product, compared to the number of images that show girls or women engaged in activities in which they are helping others, living their values, working, or using their minds. Engage your daughter in a discussion about the images you find. Helpful questions may include:

- *What do you think about the way girls and women are portrayed in magazines?*

- *Do the images in magazines match your real life?*

- *How can understanding that "seeing is not necessarily believing" help you to think critically about what you see in entertainment and advertising?*

- *How can you make sure you feel good about yourself, no matter what kinds of images you see in the media?*

There is quality media content for young girls, though it is not nearly as widely available as the airbrushed imagery young girls are exposed to daily. As part of her *Friendship Journal* for the week, your daughter was challenged to research organizations and publications that features girls in positive, inspiring ways.

The four organizations below are provided as examples of groups that support "real" girls and aim to build positive self-esteem in young people:

The World Association of Girl Guides and Girl Scouts (www. wagggsworld.org)

Girls on the Run (www.girlsontherun.org)

New Moon Girls (www.newmoongirls.com)

The Kind Campaign (www.kindcampaign.com).

Please share with your daughter information about organizations and media content that you find inspiring and acceptable.

24/7 Contact
Guidelines for Texting, IMing, and Facebook

Session objective

- To discuss guidelines for ethical social media usage, including texting, IMing (Instant Messaging), and Facebook.

Materials needed

- index cards.

Before beginning

- Prepare the *Question Cards for Texting, IMing, and Facebook* (see pages 172 and 173).
- Prepare copies of the *Friendship Journal* (page 174) for each participant.
- Prepare copies of the *Letter to Parents* handout (page 175) for each participant to take home.

Welcome back

1. Welcome the girls to the session.

2. Review the previous week's session.

3. Preview this week's session:

- ○ *This week, we are going to talk about texting, instant messaging, Facebook, and all of the other ways that girls keep in constant touch with one another.*

- ○ *Stand up if you:*

  - *have your own cell phone*

  - *use a parent's cell phone*

  - *have ever sent a text message*

  - *use instant messaging to chat with friends online*

  - *have an account on Facebook or another social networking site.*

- ○ *Some kids enjoy using social media, while others choose not to get involved with it at all. For all kids, it is a personal and family decision when to begin using technology and social media.*

- ○ *Today, we are going to talk about using technology in ways that contribute to* Real Friendships. *You will suggest your own set of guidelines for making sure that girls use technology in ethical ways.*

24/7 Contact: Guidelines for Texting, IMing, and Facebook

The reasons for allowing a child to first carry a cell phone, chat online and/or establish a social media account vary widely from family to family. Since it is a near-certainty that girls will explore these social media tools at some point in their childhood or adolescence, it is critical to open a dialogue with girls about how to use technology in ethical, values-based ways.

This activity is designed to encourage girls to discuss guidelines for ethical social media usage and receive group feedback in an engaging way.

1. Arrange the girls in a seated circle. One at a time, allow each girl to draw a question card (see *Question Cards for Texting, IMing, and Facebook*, pages 172 and 173) and offer their response to the group. Encourage other group members to comment on the question and add their own unique perspective, experience, and suggestions.

2. Continue the activity until each girl has had the opportunity to answer at least one question.

3. The facilitator should go first, to role model a helpful response and should participate in the group discussion in such a way as to encourage respectful dialogue.

4. It may be helpful for the facilitator to "take notes" during the activity by flipcharting important points of group agreement, such as "ground rules for texting" or "common abbreviations."

5. Wrap up the discussion by encouraging girls to consistently consider their values when texting, IMing and posting items on social networking sites like Facebook. Likewise, remind girls to use all of the skills they have learned in the *Real Friendship* group—such as *Stopping Rumors and Gossip, STANding up to Bullying,* and *Becoming an Ally*—to stop cyber-bullying whenever they know it is occurring.

6. While it is important to keep the age of participants in mind, it is never too early to talk about how important it is for girls to use technology in ethical ways and how destructive (even life-threatening) cyber-bullying can be. In the context of an engaging group discussion and use of question cards, the facilitator should be sure to underscore how essential it is for girls to use technology with great care and to ban any type of bullying through texting, IMing, Facebook, or other social media.

Session conclusion

- *Today, we each had the chance to answer a question about common uses of technology and social media. You had the chance to offer your opinions and hear the thoughts of your peers.*

- *Social media can be a great tool for connecting with friends, but also a dangerous weapon for bullying.*

- *It is up to you to make sure that you use technology in ethical, friendship-building ways and that you STANd up when you see others mis-using it.*

Friendship Journal

1. Hand out the *Friendship Journal* (page 174).

2. Topic: *Choose one of the questions discussed during group today. Use your* Friendship Journal *to write about your own personal response to the question.*

3. The purpose of this assignment is to allow girls to respond in depth to a selected issue related to texting, IMing, Facebook, or other use of technology, as it relates to friendship.

✓

Activity: Question Cards for Texting, IMing, and Facebook

Facilitator notes

Prior to the session, cut the questions below into individual strips or glue them onto index cards. The questions may be changed to customize them for a group's purposes. Additional questions can be written to match the activity to a group's age and level.

- At what age do you think a girl should be allowed to have a cell phone? Why?

- What are some reasons why a girl might want a cell phone? What are some reasons she might *need* a cell phone?

- What are good reasons to send text messages to friends? What are some uses of texting that are not so friendly?

- Imagine that you are a parent and you have decided to let your daughter have her own cell phone. List three rules your daughter would have to follow in order to keep the privilege of using a cell phone.

- If you could give your friends three suggestions for texting according to *Real Friendship* rules, what would they be?

- Is there any kind of text that would never be okay to send?

- If you received a gossiping or rumor-spreading text message, what would you do?

- If someone sent you a text message with a *Shredder* or other mean or threatening message, what could you do?

- Have you ever written something in a text message or posted something online that you know you would never say to someone's face? How did technology make it easier for you to say something unkind?

- Have you ever sent a text message or posted something online that you wished you could take back? How did you try to fix your mistake?

- Have you ever made a three-way call in which one person was not aware that a third person was listening in on the line? Have you ever been the target of other girls using three-way calling without telling you?

- Do you ever try to delete or hide instant messages from your parents? Why?

- Do parents have the right to read a child's texts, instant messages, or Facebook accounts? Why?

- What do you think is the right age for kids to have their own Facebook account? Why?

- Name two ways that Facebook can be used by kids to build real friendships. Name two ways that Facebook can be destructive to real friendships.

- What are some of the most common abbreviations you use when texting and IMing with friends? What do these abbreviations mean?

- How can relying on technology to communicate with friends help your friendships? How can it hurt your ability to connect with others?

✓

Friendship Journal

Choose one of the questions discussed during group today. Use your *Friendship Journal* to write about your own personal response to the question.

Letter to Parents

Dear Parents,

This week, in the *Real Friendship* group, your daughter shared in a group discussion about how to use technology in ways that contribute to positive relationships. While the reasons for first allowing a child to carry a cell phone, chat online and/or establish a social media account vary widely from family to family, it is a near-certainty that girls will explore these social media tools in their tween and teen years (if not even before). The group discussion is designed to encourage girls to discuss guidelines for ethical social media usage and receive group feedback in an engaging way.

At home, you set the standards for when and how your daughter will use technology and social media. Ask her to share with you the topics that were discussed in group today. In turn, share your perspective and family rules for use of cell phones, instant messaging, and social networking sites. Some of the questions discussed in group that might also be good fodder for at-home discussion include:

- At what age should a girl be allowed to have a cell phone? Why?

- What are some reasons why a girl might *want* a cell phone? What are some reasons she might *need* a cell phone?

- What are good reasons to send text messages to friends? What are some uses of texting that are not so friendly?

- Is there any kind of text that would never be okay to send?

- If you received a threatening or rumor-spreading text message, what would you do?

- Have you ever written something in a text message or posted something online that you know you would never say to someone's face? How did technology make it easier for you to say something unkind?

- Have you ever sent a text message or posted something online that you wished you could take back? How did you try to fix your mistake?

- Do parents have the right to read a child's texts, instant messages, or Facebook accounts? Why?

- What do you think is the right age for kids to have their own Facebook account? Why?

- What are some of the most common abbreviations you use when texting and IMing with friends? What do these abbreviations mean?

References

Anthony, M. and Lindert, R. (2010) *Little Girls Can Be Mean: Four Steps to Bully-Proof Girls in the Early Grades*. New York: St. Martin's Griffen.

Al Abdullah, Her Majesty Queen Rania (2010) *The Sandwich Swap*. New York: Disney Hyperion Books.

Bateman, T. (2004) *The Bully Blockers Club*. Chicago: Albert Whitman and Company.

Brown, L.M. (2003) *Girlfighting: Betrayal and Rejection Among Girls*. New York: New York University Press.

Coloroso, B. (2008) *The Bully, the Bullied, and the Bystander: From Pre-School to High School—How Parents and Teachers Can Help Break the Cycle of Violence*. New York: HarperCollins Publishers.

Cuyler, M. (2007) *Kindness is Cooler, Mrs. Ruler*. New York: Simon and Schuster Children's Publishing.

Cuyler, M. (2009) *Bullies Never Win*. New York: Simon and Schuster Children's Publishing.

Kroll, S. (2006) *Jungle Bullies*. New York: Marshall Cavendish.

Long, N., Long, J., and Whitson, S. (2009) *The Angry Smile: The Psychology of Passive Aggressive Behavior in Families, Schools, and Workplaces*, 2nd edn. Texas: Pro-ED.

Ludwig, T. (2004) *My Secret Bully*. Berkeley, CA: Tricycle Press.

Otoshi, K. (2008) *One*. San Raphael, CA: KO Kids Books.

Seskind, S. and Shamblin, A. (2002) *Don't Laugh at Me*. Berkeley, CA: Tricycle Press.

Shulman, L. (2008) *The Skills of Helping Individuals, Families, Groups and Communities*, 6th edn. Stamford, CN: Cengage Learning.

Simmons, R. (2009) *The Curse of the Good Girl: Raising Authentic Girls with Courage and Confidence*. New York: Penguin Books.

Simmons, R. (2002) *Odd Girl Out: The Hidden Culture of Aggression in Girls*. Orlando, FL: Harcourt, Inc.

Simmons, R. (2011) *Odd Girl Out: The Hidden Culture of Aggression in Girls*. New York: Mariner Books.

Whitson, S. (2011) *How to Be Angry: An Assertive Anger Expression Group Guide for Kids and Teens*. London: Jessica Kingsley Publishers.

Wiseman, R. (2009) *Queen Bees and Wannabees: Helping Your Daughter Survive Cliques, Gossip, Boyfriends, and the New Realities of Girl World*. New York: Three Rivers Press.